1 MONTH OF
FREE
READING

at

www.ForgottenBooks.com

By purchasing this book you are eligible for one month membership to ForgottenBooks.com, giving you unlimited access to our entire collection of over 1,000,000 titles via our web site and mobile apps.

To claim your free month visit:

www.forgottenbooks.com/free268584

ISBN 978-0-331-72785-2
PIBN 10268584

FIRST REPORT

OF THE

AGENTS OF THE COMMONWEALTH

FOR

THE COMMONWEALTH FLATS

AT SOUTH BOSTON.

JANUARY, 1877.

BOSTON:

ALBERT J. WRIGHT, STATE PRINTER,

79 MILK STREET (CORNER OF FEDERAL).

1877.

Rec. March 28, 1904.

Commonwealth of Massachusetts.

EXECUTIVE DEPARTMENT, BOSTON, January 23, 1877.

To the Honorable the Senate and the House of Representatives.

I have the honor herewith to transmit, for the information and use of the General Court, the Annual Report for the year 1876 of the Agents of the Commonwealth for the Commonwealth Flats at South Boston.

I also transmit the Report for the year 1876 of the Inspector-General of the Commonwealth.

ALEXANDER H. RICE.

REPORT.

To His Excellency the Governor of the Commonwealth of Massachusetts.

The Agents of the Commonwealth for the Commonwealth Flats at South Boston, appointed under the provisions of chapter 239 of the Acts of 1875, submit their First Report.

The Agents were appointed on the fourth day of August, and organized on the third day of September, 1875. Being unable to obtain suitable rooms for their use at the state house, or in any building in the use of the Commonwealth, the Agents, under a special order of the governor and executive council, obtained rooms at No. 5 Pemberton Square.

The Board at once entered upon extended investigations relative to the property committed to their charge and the varied business interests which, in their judgment, might affect it, or be affected by it. They conferred with the harbor commissioners, the city of Boston, the Boston Wharf Company, the various railroads on the southerly and westerly part of the city; with Mr. Atkinson, the president of the projected Boston and North-Western Railway Company; with the Poughkeepsie Bridge Company, who were seeking Boston connections and accommodations; and with many business firms and persons, some of whom were hoping to extend interests already established, others to establish new business.

In relation to some of the interests represented, the Board has had hearings, and while, for reasons which will hereinafter appear, final and definite conclusions have not been reached, and cannot be until legislative action removes some obstacles, yet many parties await only further development by the Commonwealth and improvement in business affairs. By the fourth section of chapter 239 of the Acts of 1875, it is provided that " The agents shall cause a general plan to be prepared of said lands, and shall designate thereon the portions which, in their opinion, should be devoted to railway or commercial purposes and the portions to be devoted to general purposes." After a most diligent search and inquiry, the Agents were surprised to find that no survey of the flats belonging to the Commonwealth at South Boston had ever been made, and that no map heretofore published, either by the Commonwealth or other parties, could be relied upon. It was, therefore, the first duty of the Agents to cause a proper and accurate survey of the flats to be made, and having received the sanction of the governor and council to this course and their approval of the necessary expense of such survey and plan, the Agents employed for this duty Col. Henry W. Wilson of Boston, whose information in regard to these flats particularly qualified him for the duty. His report, hereto annexed, explains the difficulties which he experienced in establishing the accuracy of his survey, as well as the obstacles that now exist to prevent the completion of the plan.

The area of the land and flats belonging to the Commonwealth is fully stated and elaborated in the report of the engineer, which will be found in the Appendix.

By the Resolve of 1866, chapter 81, and the Acts of 1867, chapter 354, a channel, as shown on the plan hereto annexed, was reserved, but by grants made in 1850 [see chapters 222 and 223 of the Acts of 1850] certain parties were authorized to extend wharves and piers across the location of the reserved channel. Upon learning of the existence of these grants and the complications resulting therefrom, the Agents advised your Excellency thereof, and asked advice and direction, and the communication of the attorney-general in relation thereto is hereto annexed. It is clear that some legislation in regard to these grants and to the reserved channel must be had before the plan can be completed. Either these grants must be extinguished, or the location of the reserved channel must be changed, or the channel be altogether discontinued, and it is for the Legislature to determine which course shall be pursued. At present the Agents are without authority to act in the premises.

Whether the reserved channel shall be retained in its present location, or its location changed, or it shall be wholly discontinued, there are and probably will be claims for damage against the Commonwealth on account of greater or less interference with the supposed rights, as they view the law, of some littoral proprietors, especially on the shore east of the reserved channel to South Boston Point. The littoral proprietors hold, under the ordinance of 1647, the flats appurtenant to their upland to the extent of one hundred rods, or to low-water mark, if less than one hundred rods.

The precise rights of these proprietors, though limited and qualified in regard to the use of their water-front, has never been definitely settled. It is still held by some to be an open question whether the State has not the right to fill her flats, and entirely cut off the littoral proprietors, without any compensation therefor. [See opinion of the attorney-general in Appendix.]

The State has, however, heretofore avoided raising this issue by providing in all plans for the occupation of the flats for a reserved channel, as before stated, which preserves to the littoral proprietors a means of access, by water, to their property. That any *obligation* exists on her part to provide such a channel, the State has not, as we are aware, ever admitted.

The State, in order to relieve itself of any real or imagined obligation to maintain a channel-way in front of the South Boston shore, in carrying out its plan for the occupation of its flats beyond, by chapter 446 of the Acts of 1869, authorized the harbor commissioners "to purchase for, and in the name of the Commonwealth, any lands and flats on the northerly shore of South Boston, lying westerly of the easterly line of E Street extended; and extinguish by purchase any claims to title in any such lands and flats." Under the authority so given, the harbor commissioners purchased from the littoral proprietors the tract of flats between B and E Streets, with the exception of three undivided eightieths ($\frac{3}{80}$) of the "Fan piece," so called, and one undivided seventh ($\frac{1}{7}$) of a lot of 165 feet on First Street, bounded on B Street, belonging, as is claimed, to Mrs. Margaret Cains, wife of William Cains of South Boston. [See petition in Appendix.] Interviews with Mr. and Mrs. Cains have been had, and it appears that they now claim partition with a view to obtaining terms not conceded by the harbor commissioners to other owners, or, as is their right, to hold in severalty, unless the State may choose to exercise the right of *eminent domain.*

It appears that the power once given to the harbor commissioners, to negotiate these claims, has lapsed and not been given to this Board.

Another matter, not, however, requiring legislation, has caused much delay : the non-action as to the final location of Eastern Avenue by the city of Boston. To the determination of the location of said avenue, the attention of the city authorities was early called by the Agents, and upon the first day of November last, the location of said avenue was determined. In the indenture of four parts, which is printed in the appendix to the eighth annual report of the harbor commissioners (see House Doc. 65 of 1874, appendix, page 58) it is provided that "said company [Boston and Albany Railroad] shall, if required by said board, take the additional area of such territory brought south of Eastern Avenue by the change from the location shown on said plan, in a strip of the same area, of equal width, along the south-easterly line of its territory, as limited by such new location; or, at the option of said Boston and Albany Railroad Company, said company shall be entitled to have deducted from the purchase-money said company is to pay said Commonwealth, the value of said additional area that shall be brought south of Eastern Avenue by such change of location, and in consequence surrendered from the amount purchased by said company, reckoning such value at twenty per cent. per square foot." The Agents have addressed a communication to the board of harbor commissioners, requesting information as to their action and the decision of the Boston and Albany Railroad Company under said provision. When the reply to this communication shall be received, and the information therein sought shall be obtained, it will be in the power of the Agents to complete the plan of this portion of the territory owned by the Commonwealth.

And when, by the settlement of these several matters,—1. The reserved channel, and the grants obstructing the same; 2. The private claims; 3. The decision of the Boston and Albany Railroad in regard to the lands affected by the location of Eastern Avenue,—the obstacles and uncertainties shall be removed, it will then be in the power of the Agents, and their duty, to complete the plan by determining what portions shall be devoted to railway and commercial purposes and what to general purposes. And it is here that judgment and discretion must be used, and such plan made as will not depreciate, but increase, the future value of the Commonwealth's property. Concerted action of the Agents, the city of Boston and the railroads must be had. It is obvious to all that the real value of the portion of property bordering upon the deep water of the harbor can only be secured by the connection of those lands with a railroad, which in turn shall connect with the several railroads leading to the West, so that the terminal facilities which will here exist, and which may be made superior to the terminal facilities now possessed by any city in the Union, may be fully availed of and so developed as to make Boston the cheapest receiving and shipping port for the trade of the great West. It is clear that it will be against the interest of the Commonwealth and of the city of Boston to permit the railroad, connecting the Boston and Albany and other railroads with the flats at South Boston, to enter upon the flats over the present track of the New York and New England Railroad, and thus to prevent communication with the eastern portion of this territory, except over a grade crossing; and it is equally clear, that some connection by a tunnel line, as proposed in the plan accompanying the report [House Doc. 100 of 1875] of the "Committee on the Commonwealth Flats," is the most desirable for the interest of all parties.

To secure some such plan will be the aim of the Agents. Already the Boston and North-Western Railway Company has taken the first steps towards its organization, but, owing to the uncertainty at present existing as to the exact lines of the Commonwealth's property, the Agents have been unable to consider fully the propositions of that company, but they do not doubt that, as soon as the legislation hereinbefore referred to has been completed, a plan can be agreed upon by that company and the Agents of the Commonwealth, which will be submitted to the governor and council for their approval; and so will be initiated the plan for the future development of the property which must result so materially to the interests of the Commonwealth and the city of Boston.

The board of harbor commissioners say in their tenth annual report that, " It was at the same session of the Legislature, at which this board was created, that a definite plan for the improvement was adopted, and it was among the first duties of this board to present to the Legislature a scheme for carrying into execution the improvement upon the basis of that plan. The plan of 1866, of which we speak, was not a plan for utilizing the flats when filled ; it only showed the extent and outlines of the proposed filling,— the walls and channels ; whatever idea was at the outset entertained of utilizing the tract of flats that should be filled, was incidental only. The project was primarily a harbor improvement." And in their communication to the joint special committee of the Legislature of 1875 (see House Document, No. 365, appendix) the Board of Harbor Commissioners say, speaking of the improvement of the Commonwealth's Flats at South Boston : " It [the State] has undertaken to reclaim them in its care of tide-water. The enterprise was conceived and has thus far been executed as a harbor improvement."

From this it appears that the board of harbor commissioners considered the utilization of the Commonwealth's Flats at South Boston as a matter merely incidental, and secondary to the improvement of the harbor, while to the Legislature of 1875 it seemed that the great amount of money expended, and the large value of the property itself required the appointment of a board for the utilizing of the flats, whose duty it should be *primarily*, and not incidentally, to prepare, report, and, with the approval of the governor and council, adopt such plan for the use and disposal of the property as should be for the interest of the Commonwealth and the people of the State. Therefore, the Legislature, without depriving the board of harbor commissioners of any portion of their rights or duties in the control and care of the harbor, passed the Act, chapter 239 of 1875, creating the Agents for the Commonwealth Flats' at South Boston, and imposed upon them the duties and powers therein provided. Thus it is that the Commonwealth has now two boards,—one to guard and protect its harbors throughout the Commonwealth, and one to protect and care for its land and flats at South Boston. The duties of the two do not conflict. Each is required, and each has its specific duties to perform.

The territory committed to the charge of the Agents has a vast area and great value. In considering the uses to which this vast property may be applied, we must call to mind the great changes in the course of trade within a few years. Formerly Boston had a large trade with the Indies and other less remote ports of the world, and a coasting trade with our Southern and Eastern ports, carried on by comparatively small vessels, bringing small cargoes, and requiring small storage-room. Cotton came by the cargo and to many parties, was received by truckmen, teamed across the city and delivered to the various railroads leading to the manufacturing cities and towns in this and the neighboring States. Grain and lumber came in small cargoes and were landed at the wharves or stores of the consignees. Then narrow piers and narrow docks sufficed, and only small warehouses were required; and the piers, warehouses and docks in Boston were constructed to meet the requirements of trade which then existed. The railroad communication directly with wharves was of comparatively little importance, as no trade in staples from the great West then existed in Boston, and no large exportation of articles in bulk was made. But now the whole course of business has changed. By the construction of railroads, communication with the West and South has largely increased, and steamers of large size now do the business formerly done by small sailing vessels. The docks, wharves and warehouses, well adapted for trade as it was carried on when these were built, are no longer suitable for the trade of to-day, when wharves to be of value must always be the termini of railroads and must be large and commodious, with wide and deep docks, with elevators for the handling of grain, commodious storehouses, and so situated that the cost of transfer from either steamers or cars must be small and the means of transfer the best, and at the point of connection there must be large shifting-grounds. But in the city proper, it is impossible to arrange the wharves, docks and warehouses so as to accommodate this changed condition of trade. The wharves, each of them of limited capacity, are owned by different proprietors, and beyond the lines of the wharves and docks none have surplus land which can be used as shifting-ground. The streets of the city, too contracted for the use of the public and steam railroads, prevent the approach to the wharves except over grade crossings, so dangerous and so constantly causing delays, which are both costly and inconvenient. In East Boston there are large wharves connected with railroads, with an elevator and proper warehouses and capacious docks, but the business of this year has exceeded their capacity and more room is now required.

Fortunately, by the improvement made in the channel, under the direction of the Harbor Commissioners, and to which the property at South Boston belonging to the Commonwealth has so largely contributed, this property is now on the edge of the deep channel of the harbor, and by its situation exactly meets the present requirements of trade. Ample piers and docks can be constructed, an easy connection can be made with the railroads, and there is ample room for the large warehouses which will be needed, and for the large shifting-grounds so indispensable at a railroad terminus; and by proper care everything can be arranged to ensure the handling and transfer of merchandise at the lowest cost. A railroad corporation already organized to build the branch connecting with the railroads leading west, north and south, is ready to build its road, if it can secure the necessary depot grounds, and the harbor improvements, already begun, will furnish much of the material required for filling the flats of the Commonwealth.

The duty assigned to the Agents is to complete the plan which will satisfy both the governor and council, the parties interested in the railroads and steamship lines, and the city of Boston; and that duty can be performed as soon as the obstacles now existing to the completion of the plan, and hereinbefore referred to, are removed.

We acknowledge with pleasure the kindly courtesies of the Baltimore and Ohio Railroad officials, who furnished us with photographs of their improvements at Locust Point, Baltimore; of the harbor commissioners of Montreal, for valuable documents; of many of our own citizens for their interest evinced in the progress of our work; and also we gladly acknowledge the kindly offices of the harbor commissioners, and especially of Prof. H. L. Whiting, connected with that board.

In closing their Report, the Agents have entire confidence that, with the necessary legislation during the session, all obstacles to completing the plan will be removed; and that with returning prosperity in business, the railroad will be begun, land will be sold, improvements will be commenced, and that in their next report they can advise of substantial progress in the realization of the benefits to be derived from the occupation and use of the South Boston Flats.

SAMUEL LITTLE.
HORACE C. BACON.
WILL'D P. PHILLIPS.

APPENDIX.

APPENDIX.

COMMONWEALTH OF MASSACHUSETTS.

COUNCIL CHAMBER, BOSTON, August 3, 1876.

IN COUNCIL.

A communication was received from the Agents of the Commonwealth for the Commonwealth Flats at South Boston, as follows:—

BOSTON, June 20, 1876.

To His Excellency the Governor and the Honorable Executive Council:

The Agents of the Commonwealth for the Commonwealth Flats at South Boston, respectfully represent that in the prosecution of their duties, investigating titles and plans, they find in the plans hitherto made for various purposes " a reserved channel " has been laid down declaratively in the interest of the littoral proprietors. They also find that the Legislature has approved of said plans [see reference on plan submitted]. They further find that the Legislature, in 1850, made certain grants for wharves [designated with references on plans herewith submitted] that conflict with the location of a reserved channel as heretofore contemplated. They therefore respectfully ask your advice and direction in the premises, and submit:—

First. If said grants may not be annulled by the Legislature? [The wharves not having been built to the line of said channel.]

Second. If the acts of the Legislature, with reference to said " reserved channel," are so far conclusive that we may not change the location of the channel?

Third. If the State is bound to provide for the littoral proprietors by any such channel?

They ask that the opinion of the attorney-general, if it be deemed best, may be taken for guidance in the premises.

Per order of the Board,

HORACE C. BACON, *Clerk.*

The foregoing communication was referred to the Attorney-General, whose reply is as follows :—

COMMONWEALTH OF MASSACHUSETTS.

ATTORNEY-GENERAL's OFFICE,
BOSTON, 7 COURT SQUARE, July 31, 1876.

To His Excellency the Governor.

SIR :—I have the honor to acknowledge the receipt of a communication from your Excellency, requesting my opinion on three questions submitted by the Agents for the Commonwealth's Flats at South Boston, and to submit the following reply :—

First. The statutes (1850, chap. 222 and chap. 223), by which Locke and others were authorized to build wharves extending over flats belonging to the Commonwealth, operated as grants, and not as revocable licenses. (See Fitchburg Railroad Company *vs.* Boston & Maine Railroad, 3 Cush., 58, 87.) The Legislature cannot annul those grants, though the wharves have not been built : the only·way in which they can be removed, is for the State to buy them at a reasonable price by virtue of the right of eminent domain.

It seems clear that the rights granted may be taken by virtue of the right of eminent domain, because the use for which they would be appropriated is a public one, the use being "to improve the harbor of Boston, increase the commercial prosperity of the city, and benefit the Commonwealth" (Resolves 1866, chap. 81, sect. 1), by making this large tract of flats land suitable for building purposes, with convenient thoroughfares, and washed by deep water. (Talbot *vs.* Hudson, 16 Gray, 417 ; and see Tide Water Company *vs.* Coster, 3 C. E. Green, 518.)

In regard to buying up the rights under those grants, the question whether the statutes operate as grants of easements or of the fee, is a material one. I am of opinion, notwithstanding the language in 9 Gray, 520 ; 12 Gray, 553, 562 ; 105 Mass., 362, 363, and 108 Mass., 209 and 216, and the case of the Winnisimmet Company *vs.* Wyman, 11 Allen, 432, that the grantees in those statutes obtain easements only, and that the Commonwealth still owns the flats subject thereto. I have adopted this opinion on the strength of the case of Hadley *vs.* Hadley Manufacturing Company, 4 Gray, 140 ; of the language of Shaw, C. J., in Fitchburg Railroad Company *vs.* Boston & Maine Railroad, 3 Cush., 58, 89–90 ; of Gray, J., in Boston *vs.* Richardson, 105 Mass., 351, 357, and 360–361, and of the well-settled rules of law that a grant from the Legislature is to be construed most strongly against the grantees (Commonwealth *vs.* Roxbury, 9 Gray, 451, 492), and that the right of use of the soil for a definite purpose, though it deprive the owner of all useful or available beneficial interest in the land, is but an easement. (Harback *vs.* Boston, 10 Cush., 297 ; Grand Junction Railroad *vs.* County Commissioners of Middlesex, 14 Gray, 553 and 565.)

As to the second question,—whether or not the agents can change the location of the reserved channel, which is set forth in the plan for the occupation of the flats, adopted in 1866 by Resolve 81,—I understand that the channel was planned in order to give the littoral proprietors access to the sea by passing over the tidewaters washing their lands (see Harbor Commissioners' Report, 1870, page 15), though, in fact, the channel, as laid out, is in many places outside of low-water mark during the lowest course of tides, but no steps beyond the acceptance of the report have ever been taken towards making such a channel.

The powers and duties of the agents are set forth in the statutes 1875, chap. 239. By section 1, the Agents are invested with power (subject to the approval of the governor and council) to make contracts for the improvement, filling, sale, use, or other disposition of the flats ; by section 4, they are directed to prepare a general plan of said lands, and designate thereon the portions which should be, in their opinion, devoted to railroad and commercial purposes, and the portions to be devoted to general purposes, and to contract for the filling and use accordingly ; sections 5 and 6, designating the terms on which a portion of the flats may be sold to a junction railroad company, and the other sections, are not material. So that the question resolves itself into this : Are the Agents, in making the contracts specified in section 1, and in making the plan specified in section 4, to act in furtherance of the general plan of 1866, or in accordance with their own individual views, as sanctioned by the governor and council? In construing these sections, the nature of the undertaking should in the *first* place be noticed. It is the reclaiming of a large territory of flats, an undertaking which can be successfully effected only on being carried out on some uniform plan ; *secondly*, that the Agents, through whom the Commonwealth must act, will probably change many times before such a long undertaking is completed, and, therefore, it is desirable that they should all act on some uniform plan ; *thirdly*, that from the time of the original adoption of the plan, in 1866, down to the time of the appointment of the Agents, in 1875, the Legislature has carefully adhered to it, and has been very careful to express itself in such a way as to guard against the possibility of being construed to abandon it. For example, in 1868, when a sea-wall was to be built, partly inconsistent with the plan (see statutes 1868, chap. 326), the harbor commissioners were expressly authorized to alter the plan, but so far only ; and chapter 397 of the Acts of 1871 was passed for the express purpose of making it clear that the original plan was not to be understood to have been abandoned. (See Sixth Annual Report of the Harbor Commissioners, page 5, House Document No. 56, 1872.) *Lastly*, it will be observed that the language of section 1 is general ; it simply provides that the Agents shall contract for the improvement, filling, sale, use, or other disposition of the flats ; and that section 4, fairly construed, provides for a plan for one purpose only ; viz., that of showing the portions of these flats which should, in their opinion, be devoted to railway and commercial purposes, and the portions to be devoted to general purposes. It does not in any way refer to the plan of 1866 ; it neither abandons nor affirms it, expressly or impliedly. In view of the facts that it is desirable the work should be done on some uniform plan, and that the Legislature has adopted one to which it has carefully adhered for nine years, it must be presumed that the Legislature, when it provided in general terms for the appointment of Agents to make contracts for the improvement, use, sale, filling, or other disposition of the flats, and to prepare a plan to exhibit the portions of the flats which should, when redeemed, be devoted to commercial and general purposes respectively, did not intend to abandon the original plan for reclaiming the flats, but meant that the Agents should act only in furtherance of the plans already adopted.

In answer, then, to the *second* question, I have the honor to advise that the Agents cannot change the location of the reserved channel.

In answer to the *third* question, Can the State, without giving compensation, shut out the littoral proprietors from access to the sea by filling the flats below low-water mark ; or must it, in filling those flats, provide for the littoral proprietors a channel by which they can have access from their lands to the sea?

I have the honor to advise that the law on that point is not settled ; my own opinion is, that, if the question is raised, the court will decide that the State cannot shut them off from access ; but the point is so unsettled that the right of the State to do so, if it is thought desirable to enforce all its strict legal rights, should not be abandoned. On principle the State cannot, at common law, deprive littoral proprietors of access to the sea, but as matter of authority it would seem to be held that it can. The reasons why the State cannot, on principle, do so, are, that at common law the owner of land bordering on the sea has a natural right to have the sea wash

his land, exactly as the owner of land has a natural right to have
water running over it continue its course and to have the support of
adjacent soil; to be washed by the sea is a natural incident of that
particular piece of property, which the owner is entitled to enjoy as
against his neighbors, because the enjoyment of it by him is con-
sistent with a reasonable use by his neighbors of their flats.

As matter of authority, Mr. Angell, in his book on Tide-waters,
pp. 171–173, maintains that littoral proprietors have such an incidental right of adjacency to the sea; so does Mr. Washburn, in
his book on Easements, p. 294 (3d ed.). But it is to be observed
that in all the cases cited by these text-writers in support of this
proposition, it was not involved in the decision of the points raised.
But it should be stated on the other hand that in Tinicum Fishing
Company *vs.* Carter, 61 Penn. 29; in Bowmans Lessees *vs.* Wathen,
2 McLean, 376, the proposition that littoral proprietors do have a
right to adjacency, is treated as well settled; and in Gates *vs.*
Milwaukee, 10 Wallace, 497; and Harris *vs.* Sterett, 4 H. & McH.,
540, it is made the *ratio decidendi*. And to the authorities cited
by the text-writers the note of the reporter, 9 Gray, 520; Shaw, C. J.,
in Davidson *vs.* Boston & Maine Railroad, 3 Cush., 91, 105; Barron
vs. Baltimore, 2 Am. Jurist, 203 (*ratio decidendi*) and (*semble*);
Morton, J., in Brayton *vs.* Fall River, 113 Mass., 218, 230. Although at first sight the cases of Brayton *vs.* Fall River, Harris *vs.*
Sterett, and Barron *vs.* Baltimore, *ubi supra*, would seem to be
authorities directly in point, affirming the right of the littoral proprietor to adjacency, on a careful consideration of them it will be
seen that they do not involve that question. They are all cases in
which a littoral proprietor recovered damage for being deprived of
access to his land by the action of the defendant in filling up a
navigable stream immediately in front of that land, but the littoral
proprietor was allowed to maintain his action for the special damage
accruing to him from an illegal interference with the public right of
navigation, not for an illegal interference with any private right of
adjacency; just as the owner of a lot bordering on a highway,
though he has no private right of adjacency thereto (Radcliffe's
Ex'rs *vs.* Brooklyn, 4 Comstock, 195), can maintain an action for
damage ensuing from the loss of the ability to use his house in connection therewith against any one obstructing it. (Stetson *vs.*
Faxon, 19 Pick., 147.)

On the other hand, whenever this right of adjacency has been
expressly taken and considered, it has been held not to exist.
(Stevens *vs.* Paterson & Newark Railroad Company, 5 Vroom, 532;
Tomlin *vs.* Dubuque Railroad Company, 32 Iowa, 106; Gould *vs.*
Hudson River Railroad Company, 6 N. Y., 543.) It should be

noticed, that, in each of these cases, there were able dissenting opinions, based on more satisfactory grounds than those on which the opinions of the court were founded.

But the right of littoral proprietors does not, perhaps, in Massachusetts, rest on the common law only. The colony ordinance of 1647 gave to the littoral proprietors the shore (if not more than 100 rods deep), provided that they should not thereby "have power to stop or hinder the passage of boats or other vessels in or through any sea, creeks or coves to other men's houses or lands." This reservation, if made in the interest of adjacent proprietors and not of the public, either recognizes a private right of littoral proprietors to access generally as then existing by common law—a right effectual against the Commonwealth as well as against adjacent private proprietors—or gives them a specific right of access as against the adjacent land-owners only.

The language and nature of the provisions tend very strongly to show that the reservation was a recognition of a general right of access, rather than the creation of a new specific right.

And Shaw, C. J., in Walker vs. Boston & Maine Railroad, 3 Cush., 1, 21, expressly states that the reservation was made in the interest of adjacent proprietors and not of the public; and the suggestion that the ordinance was passed to enlarge the right of wharfing out, corroborates the idea that at common law there was some right of access. (See note, 9 Gray, 575; Parsons, C. J., in Storer vs. Freeman, 6 Mass., 435, 438; Wilde, J., in Sparhawk vs. Bullard, 1 Met., 95, 108. But see Shaw, C. J., in Walker vs. Boston & Maine Railroad, 3 Cush., 1, 24.)

The communication from the Agents is herewith returned.

I am, very respectfully,
Your obedient servant,

CHAS. R. TRAIN.

BOSTON, October 20, 1875.

Hon. Board of Harbor Commissioners.

The undersigned respectfully asks your Board for a division of flats bounded on First and B streets at South Boston, of which she owns one-seventh part. Said piece of flats measures 165 feet on First Street, and runs parallel to B Street to the line of riparian ownership, or one hundred rods from high-water mark.

My claim would be 23 feet front on a proposed street 220 feet from First Street and parallel thereto, thence running parallel to B

Street, the whole width of 28 feet to the line of riparian ownership, and, in doing so, I will give up the water-rights in front of said flats.

MARGARET A. CAINS.

BOSTON, October 21, 1876.

MY DEAR SIR:—The enclosed (above) petition has been presented to this Board, and I have been directed to submit it to yours, as we have doubts as to which it legally belongs.

Very truly yours,

JOSIAH QUINCY, *Chairman.*

Hon. J. Q. ADAMS, *Chairman of Agents, etc.*

To the Commissioners in Charge of the South Boston Flats.

GENTLEMEN:—The corporation proposed under the name of the Boston & North-Western Railroad Company has not been perfected or fully organized, but can be at short notice, provided there is any encouragement to do so.

The gentlemen who joined in an association for the purpose of forming said corporation, laid an assessment on the subscription thereto sufficient to cover the expense of surveys and other preliminary steps for securing a location. Having done so, they there rested, awaiting your action and a more favorable time for obtaining further subscriptions.

Their proposed line, whereby it is intended to connect the Massachusetts Central, Fitchburg, Boston & Albany, and Woonsocket Branch, Providence and Old Colony railroads with the South Boston Flats, is too costly a project to be feasible, except in connection with most ample terminal grounds. The road can only be made profitable if worked in connection with the improvement of the flats; the flats appear to be of little value or use without the connecting road. The association has, therefore, asked from you a proposition for the sale to them or their assigns of a large area of the flats upon the condition that the proposed line of junction railroad shall be built and opened to the use of all connecting railroads upon equal terms. Their expectation has been and now is that a considerable portion of the flats may be offered upon such terms as will induce experienced railroad constructors of large means to undertake the enterprise and to assume the rights and duties of the Boston & North-Western Railroad Company.

They assume that the undertaking is one that will involve the expenditure of several million dollars, and that it cannot be started without a fair prospect of profit. This profit must be sought, in part at least, from the sale, after improvement, of such portion of the flats now asked to be sold to them by the State as may not be reserved for railroad service and for docks.

They assume that the profit to the State, as owners of flats, will come from the rise in value of that portion lying outside the area now asked to be sold to the corporation.

They believe that the time has come when the improvement can be carried, as the experience of the last year has proved that the commerce of Boston will only be limited by the absence of room to handle merchandise at convenient and suitable places for shipment.

Very respectfully, yours,

EDWARD ATKINSON,
President Boston & North-Western Railroad Association.

P. S.—I append an extract from a letter from one of the heavy business houses of Boston, which will be of value, and explains itself:—

" . . . During the present year, two additional lines of steamers have been established between this port and Liverpool. The Boston & Albany Railroad is the only railway company that has the facilities for transacting the foreign steam business, and the three lines of steamers to Liverpool are obliged to find all their accommodation at the terminus at East Boston. The business has increased to such a degree as to task the capacity of the road to the greatest extent. Any further increase of steam lines to Europe can hardly be attempted in the present condition of things, as suitable accommodations could not be afforded. For the proper working of these large steamers, an immense space is required, not only for the room taken up by the cargo, but for the trains of cars required to furnish the outward cargo. The business cannot be satisfactorily and properly done in a small space. Without the facilities supplied by the Boston & Albany Railroad to the steamship lines, not a single line of steamers could be maintained to Liverpool. They are wholly dependent upon the railroad company.

" The large increase in the business has been already referred to, and here we must stop till more provision is made.

" It will be a serious matter, in a few years, if some steps are not

taken to furnish the facilities which the rapidly increasing business
of the port will demand. It is also true that superior accommodations will attract and develop business. This is proven already by
the advance that has already been made since the improvements
undertaken by the Boston & Albany Railroad have been completed.
We can point to the recent past as an indication of what the future
will be, if we only make provision for it.

" Large quantities of cotton, provisions and grain are seeking an
outlet through this port that, only a year ago, were sent to New
York and other ports. The local trade is also increasing. More
than 12,000 barrels of apples left this port recently in a single week
for Liverpool. From 2,000 to 3,000 bales of cotton are shipped
weekly to this port for transhipment. . . . .

                                        " _____ _____."

ARTICLES OF AGREEMENT

Made this twenty-ninth day of September, in the year of our Lord
one thousand eight hundred and seventy-six, by and between
Joseph Ross and George A. Lord, both of Ipswich, in the county
of Essex and Commonwealth of Massachusetts, co-partners in
business, doing business at Boston, in the county of Suffolk in
said Commonwealth, under the firm name of " Ross & Lord,"
party of the first part ; and the Commonwealth of Massachusetts,
acting by the Agents of the Commonwealth for the Commonwealth
flats at South Boston, party of the second part,

Witness :

The said party of the first part hereby covenants and agrees with
the said party of the second part, to erect and build two lines of
bulkhead on a parcel of land and flats belonging to the party of the
second part, situate in Boston Harbor, off the northerly shore of
South Boston, and bounded north-westerly by land and flats sold by
said party of the second part to the Boston & Albany Railroad
Company, north-westerly by the commissioners' line, southerly by the
" Reserved Channel," so called, and westerly by the land and flats
of the littoral proprietors on the shore of South Boston, in the manner and upon the terms and conditions following :—

First. A line of bulkhead to begin at a point in the easterly ·
division line between the flats of the Boston & Albany Railroad

Company and the flats of the said party of the second part, and distant one thousand (1,000) feet southerly from the commissioners' line and to run easterly parallel with said commissioners' line a distance of five hundred feet (500).

Second. A line of bulkhead to begin at the easterly end of said first line of bulkhead and to run southerly at right angles to said first line a distance of two hundred (200) feet.

Line one of said bulkhead to be built of spruce piles not less than twenty-five (25) feet long, which shall be driven six (6) feet apart in the line or row, and to such a depth that their heads shall be on a level with city grade "Five." Each alternate pile shall have a spur-share, well secured, bracing it from the outside.

Said line or row of piles shall be planked, on the inside, with three-inch spruce planking, well secured, and extending from the present surface of the flats to the level of city grade "Five." The piles at each end of the line or row shall have three spur-shares. The main pile at each end of the line aforesaid, or row, and a pile within the row marking about every fifty feet along the line shall be about thirty-two (32) feet long, so that when driven to a uniform depth with the other piles their ends shall show above the surface of the water at high tide.

Line two shall be built in a similar manner to line one.

These two lines of bulkhead to be commenced at once and the work to be prosecuted without delay to completion, and completed before the first day of December, eighteen hundred and seventy-six.

And said party of the first part further covenants and agrees with said party of the second part, to give the Board of Agents of the Commonwealth herein aforesaid, and their engineer or other employés, every facility that may be required by said board for the inspection of the materials to be used and of the work done by said party and while the work is in progress ; and also agrees, if at any time during the progress of the work any work shall be done or any material used which shall be considered by said board unfit and inferior according to the true intent of this agreement, that, upon receiving notice thereof, they will forthwith remove such objectionable work or material and substitute other in its place, which shall be satisfactory to said board.

The said party of the second part hereby covenants and agrees with said party of the first part to pay said party for building said bulkheads in the manner and upon the terms and conditions herein set forth and agreed at the rate of one dollar and twenty-five cents

($1.25) for every lineal foot thereof upon the completion of the two lines of bulkhead, amounting to a total of seven hundred (700) feet of bulkhead.

> In testimony whereof the said Ross & Lord, party of the first part, have hereunto set their hands and seals, and the said Commonwealth has caused its corporate seal to be hereto affixed and these presents to be signed and delivered in its name and behalf by Samuel Little, Horace C. Bacon, and Willard P. Phillips, its Agents, as herein aforesaid, and the same to be approved by its governor and executive council the day and year first above written.

JOSEPH ROSS. [Seal.]

GEORGE A. LORD. [Seal.]

COMMONWEALTH OF MASSACHUSETTS, [Seal.]
By SAMUEL LITTLE.
HORACE C. BACON.

IN COUNCIL, October 10, 1876.

Approved.

HENRY B. PEIRCE,
Secretary of the Commonwealth.

[Copy.]

Upon the request of the chairman of the committee on streets, the following vote was passed :—

BOSTON, November 1, 1876.

At a meeting of the board of harbor commissioners, held this date, it was voted, that the plan submitted to this board by John T. Clark, chairman of the committee on streets, showing the location of Eastern Avenue from the easterly end of Congress Street Bridge (formerly known as Eastern Avenue Bridge), on the easterly side of Fort Point Channel as far as E Street extended, be approved. Said plan is deposited in the office of the board and numbered 348.

Mr. Lee, clerk of committees, furnishes the document (of which the above is a copy). He will give any further information desired.

J. H. COLBY,
City Clerk's Office.

SAMUEL LITTLE, Esq.

BOSTON, December 20, 1876.

Hon. SAMUEL LITTLE, *Chairman of the Agents of the Commonwealth for the Commonwealth Flats at South Boston.*

SIR :—I enclose herewith plans and results of the surveys which I have made the past season upon the territory owned by the Commonwealth and lying north and east of South Boston.

I also submit, at your request, a brief statement of our operations, together with such suggestions as have incidentally occurred to me during the progress of the survey.

The position of the harbor lines has been determined with care, but, in order to do this with accuracy, it has been necessary to establish the former location of monuments which have long since been removed.

The boundaries between the property of the Commonwealth and that of the Boston Wharf and the New York & New England Railroad have been located, and, as soon as the filling now in progress shall be completed, these lines should be marked by permanent monuments to prevent changes or disagreement.

The shore and wharf line has also been carefully examined and surveyed with reference to the plane of mean high-water mark, and several important changes noted.

Whenever it has been necessary to locate the harbor lines for the purposes of this or previous surveys, I have uniformly found the records of their location to be defective in the most essential particulars.

In some cases the descriptions of the bases of the surveys are vague, making it impossible to identify either lines or monuments where any great changes have occurred ; in others, the monuments themselves are modified or removed, and, having been taken independently and without any reference to one another, very inadequate data exist to determine their former positions with exactness.

The draws of bridges and the corners of wharves or private buildings and warehouses have been the common starting-points for the location of these lines.

There is not a draw upon any of the bridges around the city of Boston that has not been rebuilt within twenty (20) years, and in almost every case their position has been materially changed.

I have not found a wharf that was originally used as the basis of a harbor line but has been altered or rebuilt, and in every instance extended beyond its former position, but how much it is not always possible to say with exactness.

By chapter 35 of the Acts of 1840, paragraph 2, the easterly line of Fort Point Channel is thus described : from the easterly end of the south abutment of the South Boston Free Bridge, now called the Federal Street Bridge, " the line then extends five hundred and twenty (520) feet straight, so as to form an angle with said bridge of seventy-five (75) degrees ; from this point the line is straight in a northerly direction in such a position that if it is continued straight it shall not approach within six hundred (600) feet of Arch Wharf.

In 1859, the bridge above alluded to was rebuilt and widened diagonally ; that is to say, it was widened at one end on one side and at the other end on the other side, thus changing the direction of the bridge, as nearly as can now be ascertained, one degree and three minutes, making the above angle seventy-six (76) degrees and three (3) minutes ; the old abutment was not disturbed, but it was extended easterly about $9\frac{7}{10}$ feet.

It will be observed that no particular portion of Arch Wharf is designated in this description as determining the location of this line, but in the description of line B, Acts of 1853, chap. 385, par. 1, reference is made to this easterly line of Fort Point Channel, established in 1840, and the south corner of Arch Wharf is also indicated as fixing the direction of line B. It has been the custom of engineers ever since to assume the south corner of the Arch Wharf, as it existed in 1853, as a common monument for both lines ; but line B has since been abandoned, and is no longer needed even for reference.

By chap. 310, sect. 1 of the Acts of 1864, this line of Fort Point Channel was amended by striking out all of the description in the second section of chap. 35 of the Acts of 1840, after the words " easterly end of the abutment of the bridge," and substituting therefor the following :—

" The said line then extends two hundred and fifty-six (256) feet straight, so as to form an angle with said bridge of seventy-five (75) degrees ; thence on an arc of a circle of six hundred (600) feet radius, a distance of five hundred (500) feet, to a point three hundred and eighteen (318) feet from and perpendicular to the west side of Mount Washington Avenue ; thence in a straight line and tangent to said arc, in a northerly direction in such position, that if continued straight, it shall not approach within six hundred (600) feet of Arch Wharf."

It will be seen that this Act ignores the fact that the angle at the bridge had been changed one degree and three minutes about five years previously, as it re-enacts the former angle or seventy-five (75) degrees, and it is not unreasonable to suppose that it was also done in ignorance of the extension of $9\frac{7}{10}$ feet to the abutment which caused the change of angle. This description was otherwise so defective that the laying down of the line was mathematically impossible, and it was repealed in the year 1873.

By chapter 232 of the Acts of 1873, the Act of 1840 was still further amended, commencing at the north-west corner of Thatcher's small wharf, and substituting the following :—

"Thence easterly in a straight line, parallel to the line of solid filling of the north-easterly side of the wharf of the South Boston Iron Company, on the easterly side of Federal Street Bridge, a distance of five hundred and twenty (520) feet; thence north-easterly on an arc of a circle of three hundred (300) feet radius to a point three hundred and eighteen (318) feet from the west side of Mount Washington Avenue, measured on a line perpendicular thereto; thence in a straight line and tangent to said arc in such northerly direction that if continued straight it shall not approach within six hundred (600) feet of Arch Wharf."

Immediately after this change was made, the Iron Company, who owned the above wharf, having obtained permission from the harbor commissioners to extend their wharf to the new line, took up the old sea-wall, placing it further towards the new line, and there are now no public records or surveys that would enable any one to run out this line with any degree of accuracy. As the primary objection in making this modification is known to be the alteration of the line crossing the Federal Street Bridge and its junction with the easterly line of Fort Point Channel, by a curve instead of an abrupt angle, it has been assumed that no change was contemplated in the location of the said easterly line, although this line cannot possibly be established from any of the descriptions now legally in force on the statute-book, and the only method that can be adopted, should a question arise, is to assume Fort Point Channel as a correct basis, and put in the rest by inversion. The corner of Arch Wharf has also been obliterated; this wharf has been so rebuilt and extended as to be continuous with the adjacent wharf, and they are now one property; being a pile structure, in the rebuilding, it has been crowded considerably over the harbor line, and the destruction of old buildings and monuments by the widening of Atlantic Avenue, make it exceedingly difficult to re-establish; but by running out some old surveys, and comparing those that were made from 1853 to 1855, with some made more recently, a point has been determined which cannot be more than one-tenth of a foot from the true position of the south corner of the old wharf, and is now indicated only by a spike driven into the covering of the wharf. It should be marked in some more permanent manner.

Line A established as the extreme line of solid filling by chapter 385 of the Acts of 1853, extended from the south corner of Bull's wharf to a point on the easterly line of P Street, twenty-four hundred (2,400) feet northward from Fourth Street; this latter point is capable of being located with precision, but the wharf was not a structure of a permanent character, and is nearly obliterated; the corner was not out to the exterior line on Fort Point Channel, and is rendered still more obscure by being covered by the tracks of the New York & New England Railroad; during the fire and by subsequent widenings of streets, many points were removed that had been noted in surveys with relation to it, and the constant changes going on in this locality are yearly rendering it more difficult to define; its position has been marked after careful comparison of old surveys, and is probably ascertained as nearly as the corner of such an old wharf could have been observed, but the marks are of course temporary. This line is now important, as being the basis for determining the boundaries in the agreements between the Boston Wharf Company and the Commonwealth, and its location should be marked by such monuments as will prevent error or disagreement in future surveys.

The exact position of low-water mark seems not to have been of material consequence in surveys hitherto; the discrepancy between different plans with regard to it is marked and unaccountable.

In section one the riparian line of ownership falls far within the line of low water, and the rights of shore owners have been substantially extinguished, by purchase, as far as E Street; from thence eastwardly, the southerly line of the reserved channel is located upon or near the line of riparian rights as far as L Street; beyond L Street there is a necessity for defining low-water mark, from the fact that, for the distance of sixty-two hundred (6,200) feet, it is the boundary between the riparian owners and the Commonwealth; for nearly twenty-five hundred (2,500) feet, it falls only a short distance inside of the reserved channel, cutting off riparian owners from it; the area belonging to the State thus interposed between the shore owners and the reserved channel is approximately two hundred and thirty-four thousand (234,000) square feet.

Between L and O Streets occasional dredging has been done where the shore has been used for ship building, and in 1871 a large quantity of material was taken from Fort Hill and dumped upon the flats belonging to the city of Boston, in front of the city institutions, and extending not only beyond low-water mark, but into the limits of the reserved channel; just how far or how much these changes affect the ancient line of low water cannot now be accurately determined by the surveys, and the question likely to arise should be anticipated as far as possible and settled before any further changes are permitted.

East of O Street and around the Point, the line of mean low water has been carefully located by observations; this was all that it was practicable to do this season.

The plane of low-water spring tides is 1.90 feet lower than that of mean low water, but so gradual is the slope of the flats, that it can only be determined and surveyed by careful soundings with a rod.

The attention of the Board was early called to the fact that two grants of flats had been made to riparian owners which extended across the reserved channel, as located on the various plans of the harbor commissioners. These grants were made in 1850, and have been only partially improved in one case, that of the grant to Samuel Leeds and others. By the terms of this grant, five hundred (500) feet of the northerly portion is to be a pile structure. Of this, about forty-five thousand (45,000) square feet would lie northerly of the reserved channel, and eighty-seven thousand nine hundred (87,900) feet within it, making one hundred and thirty-three thousand (133,000) square feet beyond the southerly line of the said channel, and altogether beyond the line of low-water mark of spring tides. Nothing has been done under this grant beyond low-water mark.

By the terms of the grant made to Dunham and others, four hundred (400) feet of the northerly portion was to be a pile structure; thirteen thousand seven hundred and fifty (13,750) square feet of this grant lie northerly of the reserved channel, and ninety-one thousand (91,000) square feet within it, making one hundred and four thousand seven hundred and fifty (104,750) square feet beyond the southerly line of the reserved channel, seventy-one thousand (71,000) feet of which are beyond the approximate line of low-water mark of spring tides. Nothing has been done under this grant beyond low-water mark. Appended will be found plans showing the location of these grants.

In November, 1873, a license was granted by the harbor commissioners to the Bay State Iron Company to extend their two wharves northwardly to the reserved channel, as laid down upon the plans accompanying the report of the harbor commissioners for the year 1867.

Work was directly commenced under the license, and one wall, as shown on the plan, was carried out nearly to the channel, but the prolonged depression in the iron trade has caused a temporary suspension of the work. I herewith enclose a copy of the plan accompanying this license.

A pile wharf or pier has been extended into the harbor by Mr. Harrison Loring at his ship-yard and marine works between L and

M streets; this pier is six hundred and ninety (690) feet long, and extends about four hundred and forty (440) feet beyond low water and about two hundred and ten (210) feet into the reserved channel, as shown on the above plans. I find no authority for its existence.

The commissioners' lines around South Boston Point were formerly definite and continuous, and excluded the channel between the Point and Castle Island; but by the adoption of the new exterior line on the main ship channel, which extends to the north end of Castle Island, and which is to include this channel within the line of solid filling, the southerly lines are left undetermined. Some of the plans that have been made show a projection of Fourth Street, across to Castle Island, and represent that as the southerly boundary. It seems to be desirable to modify the lines of Old Harbor Bay from M Street, easterly to the Island; the lines already established lie very near to the shore. To extend them toward the southern end of Castle Island will leave an indentation in the line, which is not required by any physical condition of the bay, and cannot serve any good purpose.

The southerly shore of South Boston is rapidly coming into use, and is attracting attention for its facilities for the minor class of shipping and yachts; if this were not the case, it might seem a little premature to suggest any alteration of these lines, as the time is so remote when we may reasonably anticipate that the flats upon the north shore shall be fully improved and occupied; but along the southerly shore of the Point, important changes have been made yearly, and the lines should be placed as far towards deep water as circumstances will permit.

A line running from the present line, at the extension of M Street to the southerly end of Castle Island, would give a more finished boundary to the general plan of improvement and a more favorable line for the use of the shore for all commercial purposes, besides adding nearly two million (2,000,000) square feet to the amount to be enclosed for improvement at a point where it will be most needed at an early day.

	Square feet.	
The gross area of flats, filled and unfilled, within the lines, belonging to the Commonwealth, . . .		35,357,740
Deduct area bounded by the Boston & Albany Railroad, ...	1,907,680	
Extension of B Street, . . .	34,640	
" of E "	61,000	
Location of Eastern Avenue, . .	179,400	
Reserved channel, ...	2,008,500	4,191,220
Leaving net area, ...		31,166,520

Divided substatially as follows :—

		Square feet.
Section one to E Street, ...	.	9,222,520
" two, ...	.	9,334,000
" three, ...	.	12,610,000
		31,166,520

Of the whole area, excluding the portions held by the Boston & Albany Railroad, there is within an arc of a circle drawn with a radius of—

	Square feet.
One-half of a mile from the new post-office, . .	84,000
One-half and three-fourths of a mile, ...	1,058,820
Three-fourths and one mile, ...	3,151,700
One mile and one and one-fourth mile, . . .	6,606,600
One and one-fourth and one and one-half, . . .	4,552,400
One and one-half and one and three-quarters, . .	3,854,140
One and three-fourths and two miles, ...	3,008,400
Two miles and two and one-quarter, ...	3,452,300
Two and one-quarter and two and one-half, . .	5,052,200
Two and one-half and Castle Island, ...	2,629,500
	33,450,060

Gross area, as above, ...	35,357,740	
Boston and Albany flats, . . .	1,907,680	
		33,450,060

No one can regret more than myself that it has not been in my power to present a carefully studied and elaborate plan for the laying out of this territory, and many who have always had faith in its future development and value, will share in the regret and disappointment. A comprehensive plan for the improvement of this large property cannot be made judiciously without a sufficiently careful survey by soundings, to ascertain the depth and character of the bottom and determine the relative facility and expense of building heavy foundations thereon.

A few isolated examinations have been made at different times, for various purposes, during the last fifteen years, which have shown conclusively that the underlying strata are very irregular and uncertain in their nature.

The experience of owners and builders upon the filled lands of the Back Bay has demonstrated how unsatisfactory and troublesome it is to fix upon a choice corner for a costly building and find the mud beneath to be of an uncertain depth. If there is one lesson that has been taught more clearly than any other by this experience, it is, that the best time to ascertain the nature of the foundation is before the territory is filled, or the plan for its development projected.

By soundings and borings, made with sufficient frequency, the elevations and depressions of the bottom may be so clearly shown that the most judicious arrangement may be made of streets, areas, wharves and docks, with regard to the nature of the foundation upon which they are to rest, and thus it may not be found hereafter, in the execution of an elaborate plan, that a wharf or heavy storehouse has been placed where the mud is soft and deep, entailing needless expense and trouble, while, under the dock or square adjoining, the solid earth is easily reached, and the most substantial structures might be placed securely and at slight cost for foundations.

These surveys, to be useful, must be thorough, and will be tedious, though not necessarily expensive; but, as they will save vast outlays for piles and masonry, they ought to be undertaken before much time is devoted to the details of any elaborate design.

The wisdom of your explicit instructions, that I should first ascertain the boundaries and encumbrances of the property, has been more and more manifest as I have proceeded.

Investigations have thus been rendered necessary which must naturally be protracted, and have shown that there are many complications with private, corporate and municipal interests which, instead of being reduced, have been increasing year by year.

There are two undivided interests not yet acquired in the flats, which were purchased in 1869 of the riparian proprietors, north of First Street, between B and E streets: one-seventh of the Cains lot, at the corner of B Street and a new street laid out two hundred and twenty (220) feet northerly from First Street, and three-eigh:ieths of the lot known as the "fan-piece."

These interests have been held by their owners at more than their value, and above the prices that the other owners were willing to sell for. Steps should be taken either to acquire them, if their owners are now willing to sell at a fair rate, or to have these interests set off to their respective owners at once, before improvements are even planned.

The area of the Cains lot is two hundred and four thousand six hundred (204,600) square feet, and the undivided seventh would be twenty-nine thousand two hundred and twenty-eight (29,228) square feet.

The area of the "fan-piece" is disputed, owing to the uncertainty of the lines. By one estimate the area would amount to eight hundred and eighty-two thousand (882,000) square feet, three-eightieths of which would be about thirty-three thousand (33,000) square feet. By the lowest estimate, the amount is but two hundred and twenty-five thousand three hundred and twenty (225,320) square feet, three-eightieths of which is eight thousand four hundred and forty-nine (8,449) square feet. This estate is comprised in the conveyance of Jacob Sleeper and others to the Commonwealth, dated March 1, 1870, and recorded with Suffolk registry of deeds, lib. 997, fol. 2. The north-westerly line has been claimed by those interested in it to be parallel with that established in November, 1849, by the Supreme Judicial Court in Gray *vs.* Deluce (5 Curtis, 9). This line makes an angle with East First Street, laid off from the west, of 103° 25', and a line parallel with it will make an angle of 118° 52' 10" with West First Street, laid off from the east.

In the conveyance above referred to, the north-westerly boundary is described as making an angle with First Street, of 118° 53' 14", which would seem to indicate that the claim had been maintained by the parties in making the conveyance, and that it had been allowed by the Commonwealth. On the other hand, it is claimed by the owners adjoining, that this line is determined by the more recent decision in the March term of 1859, of the Supreme Judicial Court, in Commonwealth *vs.* Boston Wharf, 12 Gray, 553, when the line was run parallel with B Street.

There seems to be no indication of any relinquishment of this claim in the conveyance of Daniel Denny and wife to the Commonwealth, dated March 18, 1870, recorded with Suffolk registry of deeds, lib. 995, fol. 2.

The difference between these claims amounted to six hundred and fifty-six thousand six hundred and eighty (656,680) square feet, by careful estimate, all but three-eighths of which has been acquired by the Commonwealth; the remainder, amounting to twenty-four thousand five hundred (24,500) square feet, might be worth the effort that it would require to have a decision of the court upon the proper location of the line.

These interests, however, are too small to be suffered to impair any plan or project for improvement; and, if allowed to remain, the greater the projects or outlays of the Agents of the Commonwealth, the more valuable these interests are rendered thereby, and the more difficult they will be to acquire subsequently. If allowed to remain undivided, their owners can count with certainty upon reaping advantages without incurring expense or risk; if set off, they become insignificant, and can only be improved by large individual outlays.

With regard to the twenty-five (25) acres now being completed by the harbor commissioners, there is no avenue indicated by which they can be approached when completed. Eastern Avenue Bridge, which extends from the foot of Congress Street to the Boston Wharf, is completed and maintained by the city of Boston, but I have been informed by the city officers that it has not been formally laid out as a highway.

Eastwardly from the bridge the avenue is not built, or even technically laid out; there seems to be no agreement or authority which can be invoked, short of the interposition of the Legislature, to procure the laying out of this avenue, which is to be the basis of future development. Repeated hearings and conferences have been had with the street commissioners and the committee on streets of the city council, during the past year, which have resulted in the adoption of a plan dated November 1, 1876, a copy of which is herewith submitted, showing where the location of the avenue is to be when it shall be regularly laid out as a highway.

This avenue lies more than six hundred and twenty-four (624) feet south of the most valuable part of the Commonwealth's territory, lying at the junction of Fort Point Channel with the main channel, consisting, as before stated, of about twenty-five (25) acres, upon which more than seven hundred thousand ($700,000) dollars will have been expended when the present contracts are finished.

The intervening territory is owned by the Boston Wharf, and the filling of it is nearly completed.

By the terms of the agreement of four parts, dated June 24, 1873 (Harbor Commissioners' Report for 1873, p. 55), the Boston Wharf Company agreed to lay out a street for public use, in some convenient place to be determined by them, not less than fifty (50) feet in width, extending from Eastern Avenue north-easterly to the north-easterly line of the territory of the Boston Wharf Company, within one year from the completion of the filling of the territory belonging to the Commonwealth, *provided* " that said party of the third part (Boston Wharf) shall not before said time have sold for railroad purposes, its territory north-east of said Eastern Avenue, or such part thereof as to make it inconvenient for the railroad using said territory that said street should be laid out; and *provided, also,* that said party of the fourth part (city of Boston) shall lay out and extend said Eastern Avenue, or take land for said purpose, or take some other decisive action to extend said avenue, as hereinbefore agreed by said party of the fourth part (city of Boston) within six months from the date of these presents."

As the filling which was to have been completed by the 1st of October, 1876, is not yet finished, the year has not commenced within which this street is to be laid out, if it shall not be held that

the failure of the Commonwealth to fill its territory, releases the
Boston Wharf Company from its obligation altogether.

I am unable to find that any taking of lands or decisive action to
extend said avenue was had within the prescribed six months, and so
the right to this street may have to be obtained by further negotiation.

Northern Avenue is projected, and the city of Boston is under an
agreement to build a bridge from the end of Oliver Street across
Fort Point Channel to connect with it, when the Boston & Albany
Railroad shall have completed the filling of its flats.

It will thus be seen that the speedy fulfilment of their contract
upon the part of the Boston & Albany Railroad Company is essential to the useful occupation of that portion of the Commonwealth's
territory which is now so nearly completed.

Beside these unsettled or ill-defined matters in which the city of
Boston is a party, there are several arrangements between the Commonwealth and the Boston & Albany Railroad, provided for in the
agreements dated December 8, 1869, and June 24, 1873, which have
not been determined, and which must be definitely settled before the
boundaries of the Commonwealth's estate can be so defined as to
permit a proper plan for its development to be projected.

These are generally,—*first*, the right reserved to the Boston &
Albany Railroad to locate a road-bed south-west of Eastern Avenue
to connect its territory with the New York & New England Railroad;
second, the release of so much of the said territory as lies south-
west of Eastern Avenue, as it shall be finally located by the city
authorities, and the laying off of equivalents, according to said
agreements, upon the east and west of the original purchase.

By the agreement between the Commonwealth and the Boston
& Albany Railroad, dated December 8, 1869, the Commonwealth
was to convey to the said railroad about fifty (50) acres of flats, in
six years from October 1, 1869, and the railroad was to pay therefor
the sum of four hundred and thirty-five thousand six hundred
($435,600) dollars in three years from October 1, 1869, and was to
occupy and improve the property in the meantime, leaving the final
adjustment of the payment at twenty (20) cents per square foot, to be
made when the flats shall have been filled and surveyed, which, by
the conditions of the agreement, was to be completed by October 1,
1875.

Certain avenues, also provided for, were to be filled by the railroad, but for the flats occupied by them, twenty (20) cents for every
square foot was to be deducted in the final settlement from the payment to be made to the State.

By the agreement made on the 24th of June, 1873, between the
Commonwealth, the city of Boston, the Boston & Albany Railroad,

and the Boston Wharf Company, the time for completing the filling
was extended to October 1, 1876, and between the Commonwealth
and the Boston & Albany Railroad, it was agreed that they should
mutually release each other from all their obligations relative to so
much of the parcel of flats described in the foregoing agreement as
lies south-west of the south-west line of Eastern Avenue, as the same
shall be located by previous agreements; the railroad company
agrees to release these flats, except a strip not exceeding forty (40)
feet in width, which was to be reserved as a road-bed for tracks
south-west of Eastern Avenue, and to receive in exchange for the
flats so released an area two-fifths ($\frac{2}{5}$) as large in a strip of equal
width, adjoining the north-west boundary of the remaining flats of
the Boston & Albany Railroad, extending from the flats of the
Boston Wharf Company to the channel.

It was further agreed, between the same parties, that if the location of Eastern Avenue should be farther north than is indicated
upon the plan accompanying the fourth report of the harbor commissioners, an area equal to the additional territory brought south of
Eastern Avenue by the change shall be set off next adjoining to the
south-east boundary of the remaining flats of the railroad company;
or an amount equal to twenty (20) cents per square foot is to be
deducted from the purchase-money at the option of the said railroad
company.

None of the things required to be done by these agreements have
been completed. The filling is unfinished, the road-bed is not
located, and the proper apportionment of the flats to be relinquished
is still undetermined.

The new location of Eastern Avenue has just been decided upon
and approved by the harbor commissioners and the governor and
council, although its official laying out is still delayed; how much of
the area which remains south of it should be set off on one side or
the other of the railroad company's flats is not clearly understood,
owing to an ambiguity as to what is to be assumed as the original
location of Eastern Avenue.

The lines drawn upon the plan, giving the results of our survey,
are deduced from what seems to be the true interpretation of the
action, at various times relative to this subject, and as the matter
must be met and canvassed, sooner or later, a brief summary of it
may as well be given right here.

The original Act authorizing the laying out and construction of
Eastern Avenue, was passed April 24, 1852, and, by some inadvert-
ance, it contained two descriptions inconsistent with each other,
one of which was according to the known wishes of the advocates
of the measure, that it should be parallel with West Broadway.

By the terms of the grant of flats made to the Boston Wharf Company, the city of Boston was authorized to lay out necessary streets upon the granted premises; among the streets laid out under this Act was Eastern Avenue, which was described in effect as parallel with West Broadway.

In the relocation of the streets of South Boston, passed by the board of aldermen, and approved by the mayor, November 17, 1868, it was again described as parallel with, and eleven hundred and fifty (1,150) feet distant, northerly, from Mount Washington Avenue, which was described as parallel with the system of streets in the westerly portion of South Boston designated numerically.

Upon the "plan for the occupation of the flats owned by the Commonwealth in Boston Harbor, approved and adopted by the General Court, May 18, 1866, and modified according to chapter 354 of the Acts of 1867," and which accompanies the annual report of the harbor commissioners, submitted to the Legislature in January, 1869, the location of Eastern Avenue agrees with this description.

Monuments were subsequently placed by the city authorities to mark the line of the avenue, so that these lines have for years been well and clearly defined.

Upon the plan accompanying the third annual report of the harbor commissioners, the location of this avenue is for the first time drawn as not parallel with West First Street and West Broadway, and this altered location seems to be regarded in all subsequent agreements as prospective, nothing anywhere appearing to indicate that the parties were aware that Eastern Avenue was then officially laid out one hundred (100) feet wide.

By the agreement of December 8, 1869, before referred to, between the Commonwealth and the Boston & Albany Railroad, the Commonwealth "reserves the right, by its harbor commissioners, subject to the approval of the governor and council, to locate upon, over and across the said territory, Northern Avenue seventy-five (75) feet in width, and Eastern Avenue sixty-six (66) feet in width, and to locate an extension of B Street, as far as its intersection with said Northern Avenue, substantially as said avenues and street are shown on a plan marked 'A,' and to appropriate and devote the territory embraced within the limits of said avenues and street, when so located, to all the uses and purposes of public streets and highways, without compensation to the said party of the second part (Boston & Albany Railroad), or their successors for the territory appropriated or filling the same."

I do not find any record of any action being taken by the harbor commissioners under this reservation, or that there was any other laying out inconsistent with that before referred to. I am aware that it has been assumed by some that the location of the avenue as shown on the plan accompanying the third and fourth annual reports of the harbor commissioners, is the one to fix the area of flats to be released by the Boston & Albany Railroad, and which is to be offset by an area two-thirds ($\frac{2}{3}$) as large, adjoining the north-westerly boundary of its remaining flats; but as the records seem to indicate but one authorized location of the avenue, it has been assumed for the purposes of this survey, however, that the location recognized for so many years by the city of Boston was the true one, and therefore it has been made the basis of the computations relative to the areas in question. These give the area south of the avenue by the first arrangement, one hundred and fifty-four thousand eight hundred and sixty-one (154,861) square feet, two-fifths ($\frac{2}{5}$) of which is sixty-one thousand nine hundred and forty-four (61,944) square feet; but deducting the road-bed for tracks, forty (40) feet in width, and the area is reduced by eleven thousand two hundred (11,200) square feet, more or less, according as its location is moved east or west, we have one hundred and forty-three thousand six hundred and sixty (143,660) square feet as the approximate net area released by the Boston & Albany Railroad, for about fifty-seven thousand four hundred and sixty-four (57,464) square feet to be set off as an equivalent on the north-west of its flats on the channel.

There will then remain two hundred and ninety-one thousand five hundred and seventy-five (291,575) square feet, lying south of the new location of Eastern Avenue, which are either to be wholly relinquished by the railroad company, or an equal area is to be accepted by them as an equivalent, next adjoining their property upon the south-easterly side.

If the other interpretation of the location of Eastern Avenue is taken as a basis, the result will be nearly as follows :—

		Square feet.
Area lying south of assumed location,	. . . .	317,460
Deduct approximate area of road-bed,	. . . .	23,000
Leaving remainder to be released,	. . . . .	294,460
Two-fifths ($\frac{2}{5}$) of which is,	. . . . .	117,784
Leaving to be set off on south-easterly side, or relinquished altogether,	. . . . . .	128,976

From a careful examination of the records of these transactions, all parties appear to be in default, and the Commonwealth, as the largest proprietor and having made the heaviest outlay in improvements, is the most deeply interested in having these various unsettled questions adjusted speedily and finally.

Until this can be accomplished, it seems to be only adding to the confusion to elaborate new plans, which must, of necessity, be changed at the very outset, because of the uncertain basis upon which they must be constructed.

The question of the approaches to this territory for railroads, opens up a broad and important subject for discussion, which may well be deferred until these preliminaries are settled or responsible parties appear ready and willing to take the initiative in some general scheme for the utilization of this splendid property for railroad purposes.

I have the honor to be,
Very respectfully, your obedient servant,

HENRY W. WILSON,
Engineer.

_c ≠_

FIRST ANNUAL REPORT

OF

THE BOARD

OF

LAND COMMISSIONERS,

FOR THE YEAR ENDING

September 30, 1877.

o

BOSTON:

RAND, AVERY, & CO., PRINTERS TO THE COMMONWEALTH,

117 FRANKLIN STREET.

1878.

Rec. March 28, 1904.

Commonwealth of Massachusetts.

OFFICE OF THE LAND COMMISSIONERS, STATE HOUSE,
BOSTON, Oct. 15, 1877.

To His Excellency ALEXANDER H. RICE, *Governor of the Commonwealth of Massachusetts.*

By Chapter 213 of the Acts of the year 1877, the Board of Commissioners on Public Lands and the Board of Agents of the Commonwealth for the Commonwealth flats at South Boston were abolished, and a new Board, of three members, under the name of Land Commissioners, created, with the powers and duties of both the before-named Boards. This Board of Land Commissioners have the honor to submit the following Report.

THE BACK BAY LANDS.

The Board of Commissioners on Public Lands, before the expiration of their term of service, under the authority conferred upon them by chapter 286 of the Acts of the year 1874, had conveyed to the city of Boston that portion of the Cross-Dam, or Parker Street, which extends from Boylston Street continued, to the portion previously owned by said city; and they had also, by authority of the same Act, conveyed to abutting owners, for the consideration of one thousand dollars ($1,000) paid to the Treasurer of the Commonwealth, all the rights of the Commonwealth in and to that other portion of said Cross-Dam which extends from Beacon Street to Commonwealth Avenue. There still remains with the Commonwealth that portion of said Cross-Dam which extends from Commonwealth Avenue to Boylston Street, which may, under authority of the aforesaid Act, be conveyed to abutting parties, and by this means facilitate the improvement of adjacent territory, and relieve the Commonwealth from its anomalous position as the owner of a highway on which it has no abutting land, and no pecuniary interest in its traffic or repair.

The unsold lands of the Commonwealth in the Back Bay amount to about four hundred thousand feet (400,000). They are all filled to grade, and are on all the several streets extending westward from the Public Garden. As a very large number of buildings have been erected the past season in the vicinity of these lands, the demand for them must soon revive, and sales be effected at nearly or quite the prices obtained for lots of corresponding value. A small amount of edgestones are yet to be set on the territory, and one lateral sewer to be constructed, this last to be paid for by purchasers of abutting lots.

It appears that the total amount of proceeds of sales of the Back Bay Lands is $3,935,432.47. This includes the sum of $305,000 paid in land to the contractors for filling in the early stages of the works, and the sum of $1,000, paid by abutting parties on the Cross-Dam.

The total expenses for filling, grading, engineering, edgestones, and other matters incident to filling the lands for sale, up to the date of this Report, appears to be $1,625,-832.67.

It will thus be seen that the net profit to the Commonwealth on the utilization of these lands, allowing the lowest possible estimate for those remaining unsold, will be considerably more than three millions of dollars. The value of the lands donated at different time for educational and other purposes, cannot be much less than one million of dollars.

In view of these results, it seems proper that the Commonwealth should guard its vendible interest in the other lands and flats now in charge of this commission with somewhat jealous care.

THE SOUTH BOSTON FLATS.

The project of reclaiming and utilizing the flats belonging to the Commonwealth near South Boston, has received much attention, on account of their extent and pecuniary and commercial value, and now the process of development is fairly entered upon.

The Board of Agents built a bulkhead, the outer line of which was about one thousand feet in the rear of the commissioners' line and nearly upon the proposed location of Northern Avenue, running five hundred feet easterly from the easterly line of the flats agreed to be conveyed to the Boston and Albany Railroad, thence at right angles southerly, two hundred feet. And the Boston and Albany Railroad, at the request of the agents, built, upon the division line between their said flats and those lying on the east belonging to the Commonwealth, a line of bulkhead, five hundred feet long, extending southerly from the first-mentioned point.

The expense of the seven hundred feet built by the agents was eight hundred and seventy-five dollars ($875), which was paid out of the appropriation of 1876. This bulkhead was built for the purpose of retaining such material for filling as might be procured at a cheap rate, and was in concurrence with arrangements made between the Harbor Commissioners and the agents, and approved by the Governor and Council.

By careful estimate the filling contemplated above, has progressed as follows : —

On the area north of Eastern Avenue and east of Boston
   and Albany Railroad Flats, cubic yards   .   .   .   39,400
South of Eastern Avenue and east of the Boston Wharf
   Company's Lands, cubic yards   80,560
   _____

         Making a total of   119,960
cubic yards of filling deposited on the flats, and which gives the following apparent results :

Approximate area filled *north* of Eastern Avenue :
   To grade 1.50   .   .   .   about 540,000 square feet.
   "   "   2.50   .   .   .   "   300,000   "   "
   "   "   3.00   .   .   .   "   82,500   "   "

Approximate area filled *south* of Eastern Avenue :
   To grade 1.50 .   .   .   about 1,660,000 square feet.
   "   "   2.50 .   .   .   "   940,000   "   "
   "   "   2.75 .   .   .   "   633,000   "   "
   "   "   3.00 .   .   .   "   450,000   "   ".

This filling is now progressing satisfactorily and without expense to the Commonwealth.

The steamers and tugs plying in the harbor have, by order of the city authorities in charge of the harbor, and the joint action of this Board and the Harbor Commissioners, been compelled to place their ashes and slag upon the flats at a point easterly of the area above indicated and not included in the above statement; and results advantageous to the Commonwealth will soon be apparent from that method of filling.

The Board have not found it necessary as yet to build any extension of their bulkhead; and the non-completion of the contracts of the Boston and Albany Railroad for filling their flats, especially at the extension of Eastern Avenue, has prevented the Board from procuring any material for filling, except what is brought by water — as there is no point at which a team can conveniently or advantageously reach the area of the Commonwealth's flats, nor will there be, until the filling by the Boston and Albany Railroad has progressed much farther than at present. For this reason, the Board have not thus far expended any part of the two thousand dollars appropriated by the Legislature of the current year for the purpose of purchasing material to be dumped upon said flats, or in building bulkheads to secure the same in place. (See chap. 61 of the Resolves of 1877.)

No expense has been incurred by the new Board for any engineering works upon the flats, as it became apparent to this Board that the probable filling and opening of certain streets in advance of the general filling, and the nearer completion of the work already under contract, — especially that of the Boston and Albany Railroad and the Boston Wharf Company, — would afford such facilities for doing the necessary engineering work, as would materially reduce the expense, and render the work more perfect, and adapted with greater precision to the ends in view.

Also that in case any considerable area should be disposed of for railroad terminal purposes, then the area to be sounded at the expense of the Commonwealth would be by so much reduced. The work of sounding, in a proper manner, the principal part of the area of the flats and properly recording the results, will undoubtedly enhance the vendible value of the property, because the soundings will indicate the character and extent of the piling or other foundations any superstructure will require in a given location. After the filling, the necessary soundings would be expensive. It is contemplated having this work completed before any very extensive filling is done. This, with other works, to be entered upon at the opening of next season, will require the employment of a suitable engineer and proper assistants, and necessitate an appropriation.

The appropriation last year to initiate these works has not been used, on account of the dissolution of the Board of Agents and the interruption of its duties, and the non-completion of the works that should precede them, and remains in the treasury.

An appropriation was made by the last Legislature at the request of the agents (chap. 61 of the Resolves of 1877) for the purpose of completing the purchase of flats as authorized by chapter 446 of the Acts of 1869, and authority given to the agents, and to this Board as their successors, to negotiate a settlement with certain claimants, or to purchase certain outstanding titles, with the proviso that no part of the appropriation should be used "until satisfactory evidence is furnished to the governor and council, that purchases, exchanges, or contracts, have been made by said agents, which shall finally settle and determine all questions and controversies, the settlement of which is provided for by the second of these Resolves, for an aggregate amount not exceeding the sum herein appropriated."

The Board has continued the negotiations referred to in the last report of the Board of Agents, but find that Mrs. Margaret Cains, wife of Mr. William Cains, of South Boston, the party in interest if not the owner, claiming one undivided seventh ($\frac{1}{7}$) of a lot of one hundred and sixty-five (165) feet front on First Street bounded on B Street, is persistent in her determination to obtain terms from the Commonwealth not conceded by the Harbor Commissioners, in the purchases made by them in 1870 of the other owners in the same tract. The sum paid to each of the other six owners of a like interest in the same tract was $3,300. The amount demanded by Mrs. Cains for the remaining $\frac{1}{7}$ is $14,614.00; a sum largely in excess of the appropriation, and greatly beyond the present value of the property.

The owners of the unpurchased three-eightieths ($\frac{3}{80}$) of the "Fan Piece," have, after diligent search, been traced and found, some of whom are in San Antonio, Texas, and one in the State of New York. Negotiations by mail for the purchase of that undivided interest are now pending.

The plan of the flats, indicating the area to be devoted to commercial uses, and that to general uses, as required by the Act creating the Board of Agents, has received the attention of this Board; but the action of the Legislature in abolishing the Board of Agents, required them to suspend action in that regard; and this Board, organized in July, found it impossible to obtain the necessary conferences with business men and officials during the months of July and August, the time for vacations among the class with which the Board desired to confer; but now much of preliminary work has been done in personal conference, and arrangements and appointments for the immediate future, and the whole subject will receive the attention its importance demands.

Many suggestions and projects, that may have more or less control over the ultimate result, have been made and proposed by various parties, and received consideration; such as plans for reaching the flats by the New York and New England Railroad cut, — by tunnelling Fort Point Channel, — by tunnelling South Boston, — by reaching the flats by an elevated railway, &c.

The absence of Mr. Edward Atkinson in Europe has had an influence in suspending action in connection with the B. and N.W. Railway.

The Board, however, do not consider the delay in reporting the plan as at all detrimental to the interests of the Commonwealth, as the demand does not yet indicate particular uses for the particular locations, while the general idea is outlined and acted upon by the Board, which awaits events to suggest any required modifications.

An interview was had, towards the close of September, with the new Board of Harbor Commissioners, at which the duties of the two boards in regard to the South Boston flats were fully discussed; and it was found that no difference of opinion existed between the members of the two boards as now constituted. The contract for filling the twenty-five-acre piece, which has been in charge of the Harbor Commissioners, will be completed by the first of January next, as we are informed, and then this Board will assume the charge of all the Commonwealth's lands and flats at South Boston.

The Board has been notified by the city of Boston to attend a meeting with its committee on streets, on the 31st of October, in regard to the filling of certain streets as required by the indentures of June 24, 1873.

The Board is also in communication with the Boston and Albany Railroad Company in regard to the flats in South Boston, purchased by them of the Commonwealth, and have an appointment with a committee of said railroad company for a conference at an early date.

But as neither these matters, nor others of importance which the Board desire to submit for consideration, can be attended to before the time fixed by law for making this Report (which in the present case covers a period of only three months), it is proposed to make a supplementary statement, provided further legislation shall be deemed necessary.

> WILLARD P. PHILLIPS,
> EDW'D C. PURDY,
> HORACE C. BACON,
> *Land Commissioners.*

SECOND ANNUAL REPORT

c

OF THE

BOARD OF LAND COMMISSIONERS,

FOR

THE YEAR 1878.

o ————

BOSTON:

Rand, Avery, & Co., Printers to the Commonwealth,

117 FRANKLIN STREET.

1879.

Rec. March 28, 1904.

Commonwealth of Massachusetts.

OFFICE OF THE LAND COMMISSIONERS, STATE HOUSE,
BOSTON, Dec. 31, 1878.

To His Excellency ALEXANDER H. RICE, *Governor of the Commonwealth of Massachusetts.*

The Board of Land Commissioners, in accordance with law, respectfully submit their Second Annual Report.

SOUTH BOSTON FLATS.

BOSTON & ALBANY RAILROAD.

After the closing of the first Annual Report, correspondence was had between the Boston & Albany Railroad Company and this Board, which was published in House Document No. 21, of 1878, by order of the Legislature. The result of this correspondence was a payment by the railroad company, on the 3d day of April last, into the treasury of the Commonwealth, of $330,000, on account of the purchase by that company under the contract of December, 1869. Since this payment, interviews and correspondence have been had with the railroad company, but no settlement of the account can be had at present. Such correspondence as is important can be found in House Document No. 21, of 1878, and in the appendix to this report.

EASTERN AVENUE AND B OR C STREET.

In the last report of the Board, reference was made to a proposed meeting with the Committee on Streets of the City of Boston, in regard to the filling of the streets named above. The meeting was had, and correspondence has passed between this Board and the representatives of the city upon the subject; but no contract has been made for filling these streets, for two reasons: first, the city has not yet definitely located Eastern avenue, B or C streets; and, second, the abutter upon the west side of B street has not yet consented to such arrangements for filling said street as are satisfactory to the Board.

THE TWENTY-FIVE-ACRE LOT.

On the 17th of January last, the Harbor Commissioners advised this Board that the filling of this lot had been completed, and that they then turned over the same to the care of this Board. This letter of the Harbor Commissioners may be found in the appendix. Upon examination it was found that this lot had been filled from the line of Fort Point Channel to the supposed western boundary of the land purchased by the Boston & Albany Railroad, and that a seawall had been built around it from its south-west to its north-east corner. It was found also that it was a piece of land to which there was no access except by water; the street from Eastern Avenue to the Commonwealth lot, as provided for in the agreement of four parts, of June 24, 1873, not having been laid out, and the bridge from the proposed line of Northern Avenue to the city proper not having been built. During July, communication was had with the officers of the New York & New England Railroad, and a lease of the property was agreed to. This lease, which was approved by the Governor and Council, Aug. 14, 1878, is hereto annexed. It is a lease of the whole Twenty-five-acre Lot, at a rental of $500 per month, for one year and thereafter during the pleasure of the Commonwealth, but subject to a twelve-month's written notice. The lease provides that the property shall be used exclusively for railway purposes, and for commercial purposes connected therewith, and that no portion thereof shall be under-let for other uses.

By the lease, therefore, the property must be for railway purposes, which is in accordance with the views of this Board heretofore expressed, and in conformity with the plans for the occupancy of the territory heretofore submitted by the Committee of 1875, and by the predecessors of this Board. But the question is asked, Why was this piece of land, which has cost so much money, leased at so low a rental? and the answer to this is, Neither of the avenues provided for in the

agreement of four parts, of June 24, 1873, was completed
and open for use, and it was doubtful when they would be.
The Northern-avenue bridge could not be built until many
months after the Boston & Albany Railroad had walled and
filled its 50 acres ; and the street from Eastern Avenue could
not be opened, except by consent of the Boston Wharf Company, until Eastern Avenue had been located. When this
would be, this Board could not ascertain. Without means of
access and exit the lot was valueless, and it seemed for some
time that the lot must continue unimproved. No party but
a railroad could get to it ; and no railroad but the New York
& New England was so located as to be able to reach it, for
the present at least.

This road, being obliged to secure accommodations for its
freight, after finding that it could make arrangements with
the Boston & Albany Railroad for a right of way across
its flats, was willing to pay the rental fixed in the lease, provided it could have a lease for five years. But this was
declined by this Board, which was unwilling to give up the
control of the property for so long a time at so small a rental ;
and finally the lease was made as it now stands. To no other
party could this Board see that the land was of any value,
and now it knows of no party who would pay so much, and
agree to use it as this Board desired ; but, if such party can be
found, the present lease can be terminated in twelve months.

The lessee has been forced, in order to reach the Twenty-
five-acre Lot, to build a bridge of 2,000 feet in length ; has
laid its tracks thereon, has laid several thousand feet of
tracks upon the wharf, and is building freight-houses, coal-
sheds, &c., but has not yet secured any access to it for teams.
Its expenditures, completed and contemplated, are very large
to put upon a piece of land which is held on a lease subject
to a year's notice.

In the lease it is agreed that the Commonwealth shall
build the platforms in the docks and upon Fort Point Channel, as required by the plans of the Harbor Commissioners,
but which were left unfinished when the lands were turned
over to the care of this Board ; and it is further agreed that
the whole property, including the platforms, shall be kept in
good order and repair, and shall be returned in like good
order and repair, at the expiration of the lease. This plat-

form, which is substantial, has been contracted for (see appendix), and will be finished by Jan. 1, 1879. Its cost will be $47,700, while the estimate of the Harbor Commissioners for its construction was $79,000. The Board were preparing to construct the platforms before the lease was made, so as to secure the walls, which had moved outwardly in many places over six inches, as it was a part of the plan upon which the walls were built.

The advantage of the lease is that the property is devoted to the use for which it was intended. The State has a large territory, some 750 acres, between the main channel and South Boston, all of which can be filled and prepared for use as fast as it is needed; and this Board deemed it of great importance, as an advertisement of the property, that the 25 acres should be used as a railroad terminus. The long dock upon this property is unequalled by any dock in the country. It has a depth of over 23 feet at low tide, and can accommodate at one time any four of the largest ocean-steamers. To this dock it is intended to construct tracks, which will connect with the tracks of the New York & New England Railroad, and thence over its connections with the West and South, so that cars loaded with cotton, grain, flour, and live stock, can be brought directly to the steamer's side. All this the lessee promises to do. If it does so, and the capabilities of the property are thus shown and proved, the value not only of the Twenty-five-acre Piece, but of all the rest of the Commonwealth's property will be demonstrated as well as increased, so that a proper rental can be secured for the Twenty-five-acre Piece, and probably a paying price for the rest of the land as it is filled. But if these things are not done, and the property is not properly developed by the present lessee, the lease can be terminated, and perhaps some other party can be found who will be willing to pay a rental for the property.

But, until the filling of its land by the Boston & Albany Railroad Company is completed, the State under existing contracts cannot compel the city to build Northern-avenue bridge, and so be enabled to realize, either by sale or rental, the full value of the land, which can only be after communication with the city proper is established. To-day the State has no right to cross the Boston Wharf Company's land to reach Eastern Avenue; and if it had it would be much farther to the foot of Oliver Street than it will be when Northern-avenue bridge is completed and open for travel. The early completion of the work which the Boston & Albany Railroad agreed to finish on Oct. 1, 1876, is needed to enable the State to realize the true value of its land.

ENGINEER.

On May 31, 1878, the Governor and Council approved the appointment of an engineer, and the construction of an office for the use of the engineer upon the Twenty-five-acre Piece. This office was built at an expense of $537, and takes the place of the office on India Wharf previously used by the Harbor Commissioners at a rental of $175 per year.

Mr. F. W. Hodgdon was appointed engineer, at a salary of $100 per month, on June 1, and his report is hereto annexed. He has been employed in sounding and cross-sectioning the area including B Street, Eastern Avenue, and the space between these streets and the land of the Boston Wharf Company and the New York & New England Railroad, which should be filled before the filling of Eastern Avenue and B Street is completed. The survey of the territory belonging to the State has occupied much time, as there was a question in regard to the boundary between the land of the Commonwealth and of the Boston Wharf Company on both the east and west, as also the north and south lines, owing to the difficulty in fixing the various points referred to in the laws and contracts heretofore made. Upon these points and lines depend the boundaries of both the Boston Wharf and the Boston & Albany Company's land. In connection with the engineers of the Harbor Commissioners and of the city of Boston, these points have finally been determined upon; and a plan is now being prepared to which all parties in interest will assent. And, now that a portion of the land is filled, it will be possible to erect permanent monuments, so that thereafter no question of boundary will arise. With this plan completed, it will be possible to fix the boundaries of the land sold to the Boston and Albany Railroad Company under the agreement of 1869, and to settle the various questions as to territory which are still open with that corporation.

Filling, etc.

Inside the bulkhead erected in 1875, about 3,200 cubic yards have been deposited without cost to the State; and inside the lines of B Street and Eastern Avenue there have been deposited 42,500 cubic yards at a higher grade, at a cost to the State of 5 cents per cubic yard. The Boston & Albany Railroad has made a contract to fill a portion of its territory; and, if a satisfactory contract can be made, this Board will, as soon as the lines of Eastern Avenue and B Street are fixed by the city authorities, proceed to fill the space between B Street, Eastern Avenue, and the railroad.

Proceeds of Lands sold.

By chap. 326 of the Acts of the year 1878, sect. 5, it is provided that "all money received from the sale of lands, flats, or otherwise, under this act, shall be paid into the treasury of the Commonwealth, and shall be applied to the sinking-fund as provided for by sect. 3 of chap. 122 of the Acts of 1865."

By chap. 446 of the Acts of 1869, approved June 2, 1869, it is provided in sect. 5 that "the net proceeds of the sales of all lands purchased under this act, and of all lands contained in Sect. One of the South Boston flats, . . . after deducting therefrom all sums of money paid for the purchase of the lands acquired under authority of this act, with interest, shall be paid into the sinking-fund," &c.

Sect. One by the 4th section of chap. 326 of the Acts of 1868, includes all flats between Fort Point Channel and L Street, and north of the reserved channel.

In July, 1869, more than a month after the passage of the above-cited act, which provides that only the *net* proceeds of land sold in Sect. One shall be placed in the sinking-funds, a piece of land included in sect. 1 was sold to the Boston, Hartford & Erie Railroad. For this purchase, a note secured by a mortgage of the land purchased was given by said corporation for the amount of $545,505; and the whole amount thereof was placed in the War Loan Sinking Fund (see Auditor's Report for 1869, pp. 8, 204, and Pub. Doc. of 1870, p. 33). In December, 1871, under the provisions of chap. 372 of that year, the land was sold at a mortgagee's sale, was purchased by the treasurer in behalf of the Commonwealth for $545,500 (Pub. Doc. of 1873, p. 16), and was included in the investments of the Union Loan Sinking Fund (p. 20 of same document); and in Pub. Doc. of 1878, p. 32, it appears as land in Boston Harbor, purchased of Boston, Hartford, & Erie Railroad, $545,505, included in the investments of the Troy & Greenfield Railroad Sinking-Fund.

In December, 1869, a lot of flats of about 50 acres in extent, in Sect. One, was sold to the Boston & Albany Railroad at the rate of 20 cents per foot, making the amount of sale as per agreement of that date (see House Doc. of 1878, No. 21) $435,600; and on April 3, 1878, after correspondence with this Board, the Boston & Albany Railroad paid into the treasury of the Commonwealth, on account of said purchase, the sum of $330,000, which is the first and so far the only money yet realized from the sale of land or flats in South Boston. It is expected that a further payment will be made by this company very shortly.

By the Acts of 1872, chap. 320, sect. 4, it is provided that from the net proceeds of all lands and flats in Sect. One, the whole cost, with interest thereon, of harbor improvements connected with the Twenty-five-acre Piece shall be deducted, and the residue shall be placed in the sinking-funds.

By the Acts of 1878, chap. 237, the "Commonwealth Flats Improvement Fund" was established; and in this fund are to be placed "the moneys already received and to be received from the sales or use of the Commonwealth's lands in South Boston, except so much thereof as has already been placed to the credit of the sinking-fund;" and from this fund an appropriation was made for the purpose of enforcing and executing the provisions of existing laws, and of chap. 239 of the acts of 1875.

Thus, by the acts already passed, the proceeds of these lands are to be appropriated as follows: —

1868, chap. 226: All moneys received to go into the sinking-funds.

1869, chap. 446: Net proceeds of sales of land in Sect. One, after deducting cost of lands purchased, to go into sinking-funds.

1872, chap. 320: Cost of harbor improvements to be

deducted from net proceeds, and residue to go to the sinking-funds.

1878, chap. 237: All moneys received from the sale or use to go to Commonwealth Flats Improvement Fund, except that already in sinking-funds, and appropriations from the former funds made to complete work under existing laws.

In 1869 the note of the Hartford & Erie Railroad was placed to the credit of the sinking-funds after the passage of the law of that year; and the amount, although the land is still in possession of the Commonwealth, now appears in the Troy & Greenfield Railroad Sinking Fund, viz., $545.505.

The amount received from the Boston & Albany Railroad in April, 1878, was $330,000 00

So that, by the books of the treasury, there have been received from sales of land in Sect. One . . . 875,506 00

While the payments on account of land and improvements in Sect. One, as per p. 11 of this report, have been 1,004,237 59

To which amount must be added the accrued and hereafter accruing interest.

COST OF SOUTH BOSTON FLATS.

For the purchase of land and flats as authorized by chap. 446 of the Acts of 1869, scrip was issued to the amount of $230,000, which was paid from the treasury in January, 1875.

Scrip has also been issued, and is now outstanding, under Harbor Improvement Loan; viz.,—

Due Sept. 1, 1894 . . . . . $400,000
Sept. 1, 1896 300,000
——— $700,000

Making the whole amount of scrip issued by the Commonwealth for purchase of flats at South Boston, and for improvements in Boston Harbor, $930,000.

This Board is informed by the Auditor that the cost of flats, &c., purchased under authority of chap. 446 of 1869, was . $243,091 41

And that the cost of dredging, filling, &c., done by Harbor Commissioners and charged to Harbor Improvement Loan, was to Jan. 1, 1878 . . . . 638,728 43

And since then and to Dec. 12, 1878 . . 90,891 42
——— $729,619 85

And that, for work done in 1878 by Land Commissioners, the amount paid to Dec. 12, 1878, is $28,357 52

The cost of bulkhead, filling, &c., done by the agents of South Boston Flats in 1876, and charged as expenses of that Board, was 3,168 81

The amount of these several items is .   .   . $1,004,237 59

From the Boston & Albany Railroad Company there was received in the treasury in April, 1878, the sum of .   330,000 00

So that the net cost of lands purchased and of harbor improvements by Harbor Commissioners, charged to Harbor Improvement Loan, and by agents of South Boston Flats, charged as expenses of that Board, and by Land Commissioners, charged to Commonwealth Flats Fund, or under Resolve 61 of 1877, is 674,237 59

While the property represented by this cost consists of —

1. Flats purchased.
2. The Twenty-five-acre Piece, with dock, filling, and walls.
3. About 750 acres of flats partially filled.
4. The improvement to the harbor of Boston. By the Resolve, chap. 81 of 1866, the Harbor Commissioners were instructed to consider the improvement to the harbor of Boston as " of paramount importance in any intended occupation of said flats ; " and this, under letter of Harbor Commissioners marked F, and appended to their Ninth Annual Report, is shown to have been the prime matter of consideration in all their expenditures.

The value of the improvements to Boston Harbor can never be realized by money actually paid into the treasury ; but, whatever the cost of such improvements has been, it has been charged to the Harbor Improvement Loan, and is usually, but in the opinion of this Board erroneously, considered as a part of the cost of the land in South Boston ; while in fact the whole cost of all improvements made solely for the benefit of Boston Harbor should be deducted from the total expenditure. The balance then remaining after such deduction would represent the cost of the land.

HARBOR IMPROVEMENT LOAN.

By chap. 81 of the Resolves of 1866, the Legislature approves and adopts the plan (see Senate Doc. No. 11 of 1866) recommended by the Commissioners on Harbors and Flats, and adds " that the same, when executed, will greatly

improve the harbor of Boston, increase the commercial prosperity of the city, and benefit the Commonwealth." In
these resolves the Harbor Commissioners are instructed to
report all material matters concerning the occupation of the
flats; "the said Commissioners in all plans and proposals submitted by them always regarding the protection and improvement of the harbor of Boston as of paramount importance
in any intended occupation of said flats."

By chap. 354 of the Acts of 1867, the sum of $200,000
was appropriated for the construction of a sea-wall, to be
paid out of the treasury, the wall to be built under the direction of the Harbor Commissioners, but having due regard
to the proper direction of the currents in Boston Harbor. By
Resolve 93 of the same year, a joint committee of nine was
appointed to act with the Harbor Commissioners in the sell-
ing and filling of the flats, &c.

By chap. 326 of the Acts of 1868, the Harbor Commissioners are authorized " to fill flats, build walls, &c.;" but,
if the " harbor shall be injured thereby," then " such injury
shall be repaired by dredging or otherwise," &c.

By chap. 446 of the Acts of 1869, the powers of the Harbor Commissioners were enlarged, so that they were authorized to purchase certain lands and flats in South Boston, to be
paid for from the proceeds of scrip not to exceed $300,000.
Under the provisions of this act certain lands have been
purchased from the riparian proprietors at a cost of $243,-
091.41, for which scrip was issued to the amount of $230,000.
The $13,091.41 was paid from revenue; and in 1875 the
$230,000 of scrip was also paid from revenue.

By chap. 320 of the Acts of 1872 the Harbor Commissioners
were authorized to contract for the sea-walls and filling of
the Twenty-five acre Piece, which, through the failure of the
Hartford & Erie Railroad, had again come into the possession of the Commonwealth; and for the cost of this work
the Treasurer was authorized to issue scrip to an amount not
exceeding $400,000. The net proceeds of the sales of all
lands and flats included in Sect. One were pledged for the
payment of the scrip which has been issued to the amount
of $400,000, bearing five per cent interest payable in 1894,
and called the Harbor Improvement Loan.

By chap. 12 of the Acts of 1874 this appropriation was
renewed.

By chap. 171 of the Acts of 1876 a further appropriation of $300,000 was authorized ; and for this amount scrip was issued, bearing five per cent interest and payable in 1896, also called Harbor Improvement Loan.

By chap. 246 of the Acts of 1877 a further appropriation of $60,000 was made from the treasury, to be expended for the purposes named in the Acts of 1872, chap. 320.

All expenses for harbor improvements, for walls and filling, incurred by the Harbor Commissioners in connection with the Twenty-five-acre Piece, have been charged by the Auditor in his account with the Harbor Improvement Loan.

In all work done upon the South Boston flats, the Harbor Commissioners were instructed to consider the protection and improvement of Boston Harbor as of paramount importance ; and in the appendix to their Tenth Annual Report (1876) p. 65, they say, " The State, as sovereign, is the owner of the flats at South Boston, because of their relation to tide-water. It has undertaken to reclaim them in their care of tide-water. The enterprise was conceived, and has thus far been executed, as a harbor improvement; the value of the land to be reclaimed was only incidental to the main purpose, though it was hoped the value would be large, and would secure the State from loss in its undertaking;" and, further on, " But it would be unfortunate if, by giving too much thought to pecuniary results, the primary purpose to preserve and improve the harbor should in any way be obscured."

This explains the course of the Harbor Commissioners in connection with the South Boston flats, primarily to improve the harbor of Boston, the cost of the land being secondary ; and it also explains why the loan, from the proceeds of which the expenses were paid, was called the Harbor Improvement Loan. Under their supervision it was an enterprise having reference to the value of the water; but by the act of 1875, chap. 239, the flats were placed in the hands of a board who were thenceforward to manage the property in reference to its value as land.

CHARLES-RIVER BASIN.

By Legislative Resolve, chap. 25, of 1878, the Land Commissioners were placed in charge of certain lands belonging to the Commonwealth in Charles River, with authority to "make contracts for the filling, use, sale, or other disposition of said lands;" and with "authority to apply to the Harbor Commissioners for a revision of the harbor lines in Charles-river Basin, so called." The moving cause to the passage of this resolve was a petition of the mayor of Boston for an act ceding to the said city certain flats in said basin, for a water-front promenade, 200 feet in width, outside the present harbor lines. Upon the consideration of the whole matter, suggestions were made and urged that the Commonwealth ought not to part with the area asked for without compensation, especially as in making the grant the Commonwealth would also bar itself from ever utilizing the large area of flats lying outside of the flats asked for. The petition and suggestions resulted in the said Resolve; and while giving the Board slight powers to act on its own motion, it yet gave broad powers to act in co-operation with others, and especially the Park Commissioners of said city. For obvious and economic reasons this Board was unprepared to join in any plan for improving these flats, which would not accrue to the benefit of the Commonwealth; and therefore early sought to know the wishes of the said Park Commissioners, and to this end had several interviews and some correspondence. The final letter of the chairman of said Board is printed in the appendix, and seems to furnish conclusive reasons to this Board for not taking any action in the premises until some plan is presented by which some of the space included between the present and proposed harbor lines may be sold for the benefit of the Commonwealth.

BACK BAY LANDS.

The lands and streets belonging to the Commonwealth in the Back Bay have all been filled to grade; and all but a small portion of the streets have been conveyed to the city of Boston, and accepted and laid out as public highways. There yet remain a small area of edgestones to be laid at the expense of the Commonwealth. The two main sewers, running through Berkeley and Dartmouth Streets, were completed several years ago; and the passage-way sewers, with a single exception, have been laid. The cost of these passage-way sewers is to be paid by abutting parties as fast as the lands are sold. The main sewers are already the property of the city of Boston; but the others are still under the control of the Commonwealth, which binds itself to keep them in repair at the expense of abutting owners. The Commissioners would suggest that these passage-way sewers, when paid for, may be conveyed to the city of Boston, under such terms and conditions as may be agreed upon.

About 400,000 superficial feet of land in the Back Bay, of equal average intrinsic value with the lands already disposed of, still remain the property of the Commonwealth. The total cost of filling, grading, engineering, and other incidentals, in preparing these lands for market, up to the date of this report, amounts to $1,626,008.71. The total proceeds of sales (including $1,000 from conveyances of Cross Dam paid in 1877, and $1,000 in 1878) appear to be $3,936,432.47. This includes $305,000 paid in land to the contractors for filling, in the early stages of the work. The value of the filled land, donated for various purposes, not included in the foregoing sales, is but little short of one million dollars. From these results, the Commissioners are led to believe that the proceeds from the unsold lands will depend much upon a careful and considerate management of them.

THE CROSS DAM.

By the authority of chap. 286 of the Acts of the year 1874, this commission, under date of Feb. 7, 1878, conveyed to David N. Skillings, for the consideration of $1,000, paid into the treasury of the Commonwealth, all the right, title, and interest of the Commonwealth to that portion of the Cross Dam on Parker Street, in the city of Boston, which extends from Commonwealth Avenue to the northerly line of the Boston & Albany Railroad; said Skillings being the only abutting owner of land so conveyed. There still remains with the Commonwealth so much of the said dam or street as extends from the southerly line of the Boston & Albany Railroad to the northerly line of Boylston Street extended. The conveyance of this last portion of the Cross Dam to abutting party or parties has been delayed by circumstances not necessary here to enumerate, but will probably be accomplished in the near future. This last link in the chain of the Mill Dam complications, settled without resort to legal proceedings, will relieve the Commonwealth from what has heretofore been the subject of much conflict both in and out of the Legislature.

ARCHIVES OF MAINE LANDS.

By chap. 85 of the Acts of the year 1861, all the archives relating to Maine lands conveyed by this Commonwealth were placed in charge of the Commissioners on Public Lands, to which this Commission succeeds. Under a subsequent act, a portion of these archives were conveyed to the State of Maine; but there still remain with this commission all the records of conveyances and the records and plans of the drawings of the Lottery Lands, so called, in the easterly section of that State. On account of the extension of railroads, and other causes, some of these lands have assumed an unexpected value, and, together with lots granted to revolutionary pensioners and their heirs, have formed the subject of a somewhat extended correspondence between the Land Agent of Maine, and other parties, and this Board. These lands were sold by this Commonwealth in good faith; their proceeds were large, and were applied to various educational purposes and the general wants of the State treasury. It is therefore considered proper that these remaining archives should continue under the control of this Commonwealth, and that those claiming title under them should have all needed facilities for obtaining desired information.

Massachusetts with her large tract of land in the Back Bay now ready for sale, her valuable rights upon Charles River basin, awaiting for their full development only co-operation of city and state; and her large territory in South Boston, possessing capabilities and advantages as a railroad terminus unequalled in the country, — has a large interest in that renewed and increased prosperity of Boston which is sure to follow the revival of business, now near at hand.

The improvements by the Commonwealth of its Back Bay property have enriched the State treasury more than $2,000,-000, and there is over $1,000,000 more to be added thereto when the 400,000 feet still unsold shall be disposed of. From the sale of the lands bordering upon Charles-river

Basin, another million should go into the treasury. And from the South Boston property, the net cost of which, with accrued interest, is to-day nearly $1,000,000, the sum hereafter to be realized must be very large if Boston is still to be a commercial city. That this is likely to be, is shown by the events of daily occurrence. Look at the great increase in the business between Boston and Europe, — four or five steamers with their enormous cargoes of Western produce leaving every week, and next month still another line of steamers to be added to the fleet already so large!

It may be that the time for the large East India business of former days has gone by as surely as has the day for the small sailing vessels for which the wharves and docks in the city proper were fitted; but the coastwise business now done by large steamers exceeds in volume the coastwise business of the past, and to this is to be added the already immense and probably increasing trade with Europe, never before possessed by Boston. This business comes here because the Boston & Albany Railroad at East Boston, and the Fitchburg Railroad at Constitution Wharf, have furnished terminal facilities unequalled in New York. But these are limited in extent, and are nearly exhausted. For an increased trade more terminal grounds must be furnished. And where in Boston Harbor can a suitable terminus for a freight-railroad be found except in South Boston?

The commerce of to-day needs a direct communication with the tracks of the railroad. Great spaces for cars and large docks for the steamers must be secured, or the business will go elsewhere. The wharves of the past are useless for the commerce of to-day, and in the city proper the required spaces for cars cannot be had. It is the minimum cost of handling, and the promptness with which it can be done, which will increase and retain the trade.

At present prices of labor and material, these flats at South Boston can be walled, filled, and made ready for use, at as low a cost as was ever anticipated. In 1867 the special committee appointed to examine the subject reported that the flats could be filled at a cost of 50 cents per cubic yard. To-day a contract is in force which has been made by the Boston & Albany Railroad for filling its South Boston flats at a cost of less than 35 cents per cubic yard. Then even

3

conservative men were not discouraged, and yet the prospect for the use of the South Boston territory was not nearly so good as it is to-day.

But it is not for the Commonwealth to furnish more money or more credit to develop this enterprise: she has done enough of that already. Her credit has been furnished largely to the Western and the Hartford & Erie Railroads, and with her credit and her money the Hoosac Tunnel has been completed. By her money a portion of the South Boston property has been put in condition for use as a rail-road-terminus. The missing link is the branch railroad which shall connect the tunnel, the railroads, and the docks, all the product of her credit, so that the business of all may be increased, and the work for which all were built may be done, and done cheaply. For this branch railroad the Common-wealth looks to the business men and the capitalists, so largely interested in the business and prosperity of Boston. With so much done by the State, will the men of Boston still hold back, and decline to use the advantages already within their reach? If they do, the extent of Boston's business with the West is the business of to-day. But such action is not to be anticipated. They will at least protect their own interests. They will not sacrifice their own capi-tal already invested in Boston, nor will they fail to find a use for the land which the State has prepared for their develop-ment.

In the words of the Special Committee of 1867 (House Doc. 1868, No. 76, p. 48), " We make no figures as to the ultimate value of these flats. Tabular statements are easily made; but the prices must be conjectural, if not entirely fanciful. Men with their eyes in the backs of their heads see nothing but ruin in such an enterprise. Men who look ahead, men of faith, see success. We believe in the future of Boston and of Massachusetts; that our future will be as our past, and more abundant; and therefore we believe in this enterprise, and seek to impress others with that faith."

WILLARD P. PHILLIPS,
E. C. PURDY,
HORACE C. BACON,
Land Commissioners.

BOSTON, Dec. 20, 1878.

APPENDIX.

APPENDIX.

To the Board of Land Commissioners of the Commonwealth of Massachusetts.

The following is a statement of the work which I have done under your direction, since I took charge as engineer of the improvement of the Commonwealth's Flats at South Boston, June 1, 1878.

SURVEYS.

I first made a survey of the Commonwealth's flats south of Eastern Avenue, and west of and including B Street, taking levels over the surface and soundings to determine the grade of the hard clay. These levels and soundings were continued on B Street to within about 200 feet of First Street. The records of these soundings will be preserved for the use of the Commonwealth, or such of its assigns as may hereafter improve this area, they being used to determine to what depth excavations of piling will have to go to secure a solid foundation for buildings or other works.

In making these surveys I used the monuments which were placed by the Harbor Commissioners to mark the channel and property lines. I made plans of these surveys, and estimates of the amounts of material required to fill the territory to grade 16.

In September I commenced to make surveys to relocate the channel line on the easterly side of Fort Point Channel, and the Commissioners' lines A and B which are referred to in defining the boundaries between the Commonwealth and the Boston Wharf Company.

The Channel line from Federal-street Bridge eastward was established by statute in 1840, and afterwards modified in 1864 and 1873; but the descriptions of the changes are so indefinite, that it is impossible to precisely locate the modified line. There is, however, no change in reality of the Channel line, beyond a point about 500 feet west of Mount Washington-avenue Bridge ; and, as the portion east of Mount Washington-avenue Bridge is all that relates to the Commonwealth Flats, I have located the line as established by the statute of 1840.

The monuments described in the act are the east end of the south abutment of Federal-street Bridge, the direction of the bridge, and Arch Wharf.

The bridge abutment has been raised, and no record kept of the change, so that the relocation of its east end is somewhat indefinite   The bridge has been widened, and its direction changed ; but I obtained the record of the change from the City Engineer of Boston. No particular part of Arch Wharf is mentioned in the act but it has been tacitly understood that the south corner was meant. The wharf has been rebuilt two or three times since then; but I relocated the south corner from notes of Mr. Alexander Wadsworth taken in 1843, and by the City Engineer in 1852.

Commissioners' lines A and B were established by statute in 1853, and described by distances from the east corner of P and Fourth Streets in South Boston, and respectively by the south corners of Bull's and Arch Wharves.

The south corner of Bull's Wharf I relocated by notes of surveys made by the City Engineer, and by portions of the old wharf which still exist.

I have furnished the Harbor Commissioners a copy of the plan of my location of the harbor line on the easterly side of Fort Point Channel; and I have prepared a plan showing the channel and property lines between the lands of the Commonwealth, the Boston Wharf Company, and the New York & New England Railroad Company, as determined by this survey. And it is under consideration, to have this survey and plan adopted, and jointly agreed to by all parties in interest, so that the monuments and lines therein established may be authoritative and binding upon all parties, and so disputes and litigations may not here-after arise as old monuments disappear or become less reliable.

FILLING.

In June Mr. James Brown deposited about 1,000 cubic yards of gravel-ballast south of Eastern Avenue near B Street, at no expense to the Commonwealth.

Mr. Charles Woolley deposited on the Commonwealth Flats south of Eastern Avenue, and west of and including B Street, nearly all the material which he dug, under a contract with the Harbor Commissioners, together with some gravel-ballast which he took from the English steamers, amounting, all together, to about 42,500 cubic yards, at 5 cents per cubic yard. Mr. Woolley also deposited about 1,200 cubic yards inside the bulkhead built in 1876, free of expense to the Commonwealth. Mr. Boynton deposited about 1,000 cubic yards of gravel and mud inside the bulkhead, free of expense.

The area south of Eastern Avenue, and west of and including B Street, contains about 600,000 square feet (13.8 acres). Previous to 1878 it had been used as a dump-ground by various parties, who had deposited about 73,000 cubic yards of material on it, and raised it from about 1 foot below mean low water, to about $2\frac{1}{2}$ feet above mean low water. In 1878 Mr. Charles Woolley has deposited about 42,500 cubic yards on it, and raised it to an average of about $4\frac{1}{2}$ feet above mean low water.

This leaves about 193,000 cubic yards required to raise the territory to grade 13, which is the height to which it has to be filled by material taken from the harbor.

Most of the filling which remains will have to be done by cars, or some similar method.

There has been deposited at various times on the Commonwealth Flats east of B Street and the Boston & Albany Railroad Company's flats, about 80,000 cubic yards of material, raising an area of about 17 acres, from an average of about 2½ feet below mean low water, to an average of about 1 foot above mean low water.

This dumping and filling has hitherto been without care as to locality, and very irregular; but this season, under your direction, I have selected the localities for dumping, and attended closely to it, to secure compliance with instructions; and the result has been very advantageous in placing the material as high as possible, close up to the property already filled, instead of forming a ridge at some distance from it, as had nearly been accomplished before I took charge.

PLATFORMS.

In August I prepared plans and specifications for building platforms in front of the dock walls, and the light wall along Fort Point Channel, and fenders along the face of the heavy sea-walls; the plans in general conforming to the designs presented in the Harbor Commissioners' reports.

The platforms are supported on oak piles, are timbered with Southern pine, and covered with spruce planks. The fender is a row of oak piles driven along the face of the heavy wall, secured together by iron rods, and their heads fastened to the wall by iron straps.

After the contract to build the platforms was awarded to Messrs. Ross & Lord of Ipswich, I laid out the work, and superintended the building, which will be completed Jan. 1, 1879.

The work has been done according to the original plans and specifications, except a change in the method of securing the heads of the fenders along the face of the heavy wall, and the omission of about 37 feet of the platform across the end of the dock, which was omitted at the request of the New York & New England Railroad Company. The platforms were built in order to complete the work which was originally designed by the Harbor Commissioners, to secure a deep-water berth for large ocean steamers at less expense and in a more convenient form than could be obtained by a wall built to the required depth. Such a wall would cost at least $200 per lineal foot, while the light wall and platform together cost less than $60 per lineal foot; and the amount of extra filling which would have to be done if a deep wall was built would cost one-half the cost of the platform.

The contract to furnish all the materials, and complete the work, was awarded to Messrs. Ross & Lord of Ipswich for $47,700, to be completed in fourteen weeks from the date of approval, Sept. 10, 1878.

Respectfully submitted.

F. W. HODGDON, *Engineer.*

AGREEMENT

BETWEEN THE NEW YORK & NEW ENGLAND RAILROAD COMPANY AND THE COMMONWEALTH OF MASSACHUSETTS.

This agreement, made and entered into this thirty-first day of July, Anno Domini eighteen hundred and seventy-eight, by and between the Commonwealth of Massachusetts, by Willard P. Phillips, Edward C. Purdy, and Horace C. Bacon, its Land Commissioners, duly appointed and qualified, in pursuance of chapter two hundred and thirteen of the Acts of the General Court of Massachusetts, passed in the year eighteen hundred and seventy-seven, party of the first part, and the New-York & New-England Railroad Company, a corporation duly established by law, party of the second part, *witnesseth*, —

That the party of the first part doth hereby demise and lease unto the party of the second part certain lands and flats belonging to said Commonwealth, situated in South Boston, and known as the Twenty-five Acre Lot, and bounded in part by Fort Point Channel, in part by the main ship channel, in part by lands and flats of the Boston & Albany Railroad Company, and in part by land of the Boston Wharf Company; together with all the docks, platforms, piling and other appurtenances thereto belonging, and with the right to construct and maintain a trestle-bridge over and across the Commonwealth flats, at such place as shall be most convenient to reach the demised premises.

To have and to hold the same, subject to the conditions hereinafter set forth, for the term of one year from the first day of August next, and thereafter during the pleasure of said Commonwealth, and until the expiration of twelve months after written notice shall have been given to said party of the second part, by or on behalf of said Commonwealth, of its desire to terminate this lease; yielding and paying therefor rent at the rate of six thousand dollars per annum, payable to the treasurer of said Commonwealth, in equal monthly instalments of five hundred dollars each, within the first three days of each and every month; and in like proportion for any fraction of a month unexpired at the legal termination of this lease. The first payment is to be made on the first day of November next.

But this lease is made and accepted upon the following express conditions; namely, —

1st, The said rent shall be paid punctually as and when the same shall become due.

2d, That the demised premises shall be improved and used by said party of the second part exclusively for railway purposes, and commercial purposes in aid thereof, and no portion thereof shall be under-let for other uses.

3d, The party of the second part shall make improvements, and erect any buildings, on the demised premises, for the more convenient transaction of its business; and it may remove the same at its pleasure, and it shall remove the same at the termination of this lease; subject, however, to the right of the Commonwealth to take such of said buildings as may then remain upon the property, at an appraised value to be made by two or more disinterested men to be appointed by the Governor and Council.

4th, That the party of the second part, during its tenancy, shall keep the premises, and the property of the Commonwealth thereon, in good condition and repair, and shall surrender the same in like good condition at the termination of this lease; and shall fill all excavations, level all embankments, and remove all accumulations, created or permitted during its tenancy.

5th, That the party of the second part, so long as it continues in the possession and use of the demised premises under this agreement, shall not charge for the use of its rails by responsible contractors, between the same and any point within thirteen miles thereof, more than fifty cents per car, for any dump-cars loaded with gravel which may be hauled over its road (including the return-passage empty) for the filling of any of the Commonwealth flats in South Boston.

6th, The Land Commissioners and their agents shall have the right at all reasonable times to enter upon the premises, and examine the condition thereof; and they shall also have the right to hold, occupy, and use, without molestation, and free of charge, their office building now standing upon said property. But the position of the building may be changed at expense of party of second part; and it shall be located at such point as may not unreasonably interfere with the convenient use of the demised premises by the party of the second part.

7th, In case of default in the payment of rent herein reserved, or of any instalment thereof, as and when the same shall become due, the party of the first part may by its Land Commissioners or otherwise, without any notice or demand, enter upon the premises, and thereby terminate the estate hereby created; and in such case may hold as security for such unpaid rent any buildings, tracks, or other structures then standing on said premises, and belonging to the party of the second part.

8th, This agreement shall not be binding upon either party until (1) it shall have been approved by the Governor and Council, and (2) until the party of the second part shall have secured control of a right of way connecting its tracks with the demised premises.

9th, It is further understood and agreed that the party of the first part shall proceed forthwith, at the expense of the Commonwealth, to construct the proposed platforms and piling needed to adapt the dock and sea-wall upon said premises to convenient use for commercial purposes,

4

in substantial accordance with the plans heretofore adopted by said Land Commissioners, and shall further cause said dock to be dredged to the depth and in the manner required by said plans.

Witness the hands and seals of the parties hereto, the day and year first above written.

NEW-YORK & NEW-ENGLAND
RAILROAD COMPANY.

By Wm. T. Hart, *President.*

> SEAL OF
> N.Y. & N.E.
> R.R. Co.

COMMONWEALTH OF MASSACHUSETTS.

Witness:
DAVID PULSIFER.

By WILL'D P. PHILLIPS,   *Land Comm'rs*
EDW'D C. PURDY,   *of the*
HORACE C. BACON,   *Commonwealth.*

> SEAL OF THE
> COMMON EALTH OF
> MASSACHUSETTS.

In Council Aug. 14, 1878.
Approved:
HENRY B. PEIRCE,
Secretary.

July 31, 1878.
Approved:
CHARLES R. TRAIN,
Attorney-General.

ARTICLES OF AGREEMENT

BETWEEN MESSRS. ROSS & LORD AND THE COMMONWEALTH OF MASSACHUSETTS.

Articles of Agreement made this thirtieth day of August in the year of our Lord one thousand eight hundred and seventy-eight, by and between Joseph Ross and George A. Lord, both of Ipswich in the County of Essex and Commonwealth of Massachusetts, copartners in business, doing business at Boston, in the County of Suffolk, in said Commonwealth, under the firm name of Ross & Lord, parties of the first part; and the Commonwealth of Massachusetts, acting by its Board of Land Commissioners, party of the second part: witness, —

The said parties of the first part hereby covenant and agree, with the said party of the second part, to erect and build platforms for the dock in the Commonwealth Flats at South Boston, platforms in front of the light sea-wall enclosing the said flats, on the Fort Point side of the same, and also fenders for the face of the heavy sea-wall both east and west of said dock, in the manner and of the materials recited in the specifications hereunto annexed and the plans in said specifications referred to (said plans are in the office of the engineer in charge, and the same are signed by the Land Commissioners and the parties of the first part, and dated of an even date herewith, and marked respectively " A," " B," " C," " D," " E," & " F"), and further under the direction of the engineer of said Board of Land Commissioners as recited in said specifications and upon the terms and conditions following.

The platforms in front of the light sea-wall aforesaid to be commenced at once, and the work thereon to be prosecuted without delay; and completed in 4 weeks from the date hereof; and all the work and all the fenders and platforms herein agreed to be done to be completed in 14 weeks from the day of the date hereof.

And said parties of the first part further covenant and agree with said party of the second part, to give the Board of Land Commissioners, and its engineer or other agents, every facility that may be required by said Board for the inspection of materials to be used, and of the work to be done by said parties under this agreement, and while such work is in progress; and also agree, if at any time during the progress of the work any work shall be done, or any materials used, which shall be considered by said Board or their engineer unfit or inferior, according to the true interest of this agreement, that, upon receiving notice thereof, they will forthwith remove such objectionable work or material, and substitute other in its place, which shall be satisfactory to said Board or their engineer.

And said parties of the first part further agree that any person shall be deemed the engineer of the Board of Land Commissioners, within the meaning of this agreement, whom said Board shall from time to time designate for the performance of any service it may desire in relation to the work to be done under this agreement.

And said parties of the first part further agree that the Land Commissioners, subject to the approval of the Governor and Council, shall have the right to make changes in the plan of doing said work, should occasion arise, and make such additions to and reductions from the contract price as shall be just to both parties. It is further agreed by and between said parties hereto, that should the parties of the first part refuse or neglect to execute according to this agreement the work herein contracted for, or fail to prosecute the same with the requisite vigor to insure its completion within the time agreed upon, or in any other respect violate this agreement, the Board of Land Commissioners shall have the power to annul this agreement and to contract anew with other parties, at the cost and expense of the said parties of the first part; and in that case the said parties of the first part do hereby covenant and agree to pay to said party of the second part any and all cost and expense which the said party of the second part shall so incur in the completion of the work as contracted herein to be done by said parties of the first part.

The party of the second part hereby covenants and agrees with said parties of the first part, to pay said parties of the first part for furnishing the material and doing the work, and building said platforms and fenders, in the manner and upon the terms and conditions herein set forth and agreed, the sum of forty-seven thousand seven hundred dollars ($47,700); payments to be made every month for the work performed under this contract to the satisfaction of the engineer of the Board, at the rate of 80 per cent of the contract price of the work done during the month, as reported and certified to by the said engineer, and upon the approval of the bills by the Board of Land Commissioners and the Governor and Council.

It is further agreed by and between said parties hereto, that in case any difference shall arise under this agreement between the parties of the first part and the party of the second part, acting by the Board of Land Commissioners, that the said parties of the first part and the said Board are unable to settle and adjust, the same shall be finally determined upon hearing by the Governor and Council.

This contract to take effect upon its approval by the Governor and Council.

In testimony whereof the said Ross and Lord, parties of the first part, have hereunto set their hands and seals; and the said Commonwealth has caused its corporate seal to be hereto affixed, and these presents to be

signed and delivered in its name and behalf, by Willard P. Phillips,
Edward C. Purdy, and Horace C. Bacon, its Land Commissioners, as
herein aforesaid, the day and year first above written.

Signed, sealed, and delivered in
presence of
{ JOSEPH ROSS, [SEAL.]

GEORGE A. LORD, [SEAL.] }

GEO. C. BURPEE,
AUG. BROWN.

COMMONWEALTH OF MASSACHUSETTS.

[SEAL OF THE COMMONWEALTH.] By WILLARD P. PHILLIPS,
EDWARD C. PURDY, } *Land Commissioners.*
HORACE C. BACON,

Approved under the provisions of Chap. 239 of the Acts of 1875.

F. W. LINCOLN,
F. A. NYE, } *Harbor Commissioners.*
ALBERT MASON,

In Council, Sept. 10, 1878.

Approved:
HENRY B. PEIRCE,
Secretary.

SPECIFICATIONS

OR PLATFORMS FOR DOCK IN THE COMMONWEALTH'S FLATS AT SOUTH BOSTON.

The plans and sections on file at the chief engineer's office on the South Boston Flats show the length, width, character, and details of the work to be done.

The platforms are to be built along the face of the dock walls, and connected with the fenders to be built along the faces of the heavy sea-walls. For a distance of about 1,260 feet they are to be 24 feet wide, and the balance of the distance, as shown by the plan, will widen out on each side to 44 feet at the mouth of the dock. The whole length of the platform is about 1,840 feet. All the piles for the support of the platform and capsill are to be of oak, excluding black oak, free from decay, straight, and not less than 8 inches in diameter at the smaller end. They shall be driven to depths shown in the sectional plans ; and, whenever in the opinion of the engineer in charge it shall be deemed necessary, they shall be shod with iron. All piles injured, broken, driven out of line, or not in accordance with the plans, shall be removed by the contractor.

Piles shall be cut off at such a height and in such a manner that the timber platform can be framed thereon, as per plan, and at such grade as the engineer shall establish. Spur-shores are included in the word "piles." 12 mooring-piles shall be driven 3 feet inside the front line of the platform, as shown by plan, and at points indicated by the engineer. They shall project 4 feet above the surface of the platform, and shall be firmly braced and secured as the engineer may direct. They shall be at least 18 inches in diameter at the top, and be driven to the same depth as the front piles of the platform.

A row of spruce piles is to be driven on a line and close together 4 feet back from the front line of the platform, and to a depth of 35 feet below mean low water, and to be cut off at the top at the level of mean low water. The piles shall not be less than $6\frac{1}{2}''$ in diameter at the smaller end.

The braces will be white oak, not less than 5" diameter at the smaller end, and flattened where they bear against the piles, and bolted to the piles and spur-shores.

All the timbers of the frame of the platforms shall be of sound Southern pine, free from sap, shakes, and splits, and of the dimensions shown by the drawings. The floor-timbers shall break joint with each other.

The planks shall be of spruce, sound, free from sap, shakes, splits, large or loose knots, and shall be 3" inches thick, of equal widths, not more than 12", and shall break joint with each other.

The capsills are to be protected at the corners of the platforms by iron straps $\frac{1}{2}$" thick.

Bolts are to be $1\frac{1}{4}$" diameter, with the screw-threads clean cut, and of suitable length for the nuts to come to a solid bearing.

The nuts are to be $2\frac{1}{2}$" square and $1\frac{1}{4}$" thick.

Washers are to be 4" square and $\frac{1}{2}$" thick.

The floor-timbers are to be fastened by wrought-iron spike-bolts, $\frac{3}{4}$" diameter and 18" long.

The planks are to be spiked with the best wrought-iron ship-spikes, 6" long.

The ironwork must all be of a good quality of wrought-iron, acceptable to the engineer in charge.

Treenails are to be of white oak, $1\frac{1}{4}$" diameter, free from sap, and sound in every way.

All the work must be done in accordance with the plans and directions furnished by the engineer, and must be done in a thorough and workmanlike manner, to the acceptance of the Land Commissioners and their engineer ; and every opportunity must be given for inspection at all times. The Land Commissioners shall also have the right to reject any piles, timber, plank, or any portion of the ironwork, and to require the removal of any piece of wood or ironwork already in place which is unsatisfactory, and the substitution therefor of good material, and satisfactory to the Land Commissioners.

SPECIFICATIONS

FOR PLATFORMS TO BE BUILT IN FRONT OF LIGHT SEA-WALL ENCLOSING THE COMMONWEALTH'S FLATS AT SOUTH BOSTON.

The plans and sections on file at the chief engineer's office, on South Boston Flats, show the length, width, character, and details of the work to be done.

The platforms are to be 29 feet wide ; and the length is 312.5 feet on a straight line, and 396 feet on a curve, measured on the front line ; and they are to be connected with the fender to be built along the face of the heavy sea-wall.

All piles for the support of the platform and capsill are to be 40 feet long, of oak, excluding black oak, free from decay, straight, and not less than 8 inches diameter at the smaller end. Spur-shores are to be of the same quality, 30 feet long, and not less than 8 inches diameter at the smaller end ; and all piles and spur-shores are to be driven and secured as shown by sectional drawings. Whenever, in the opinion of the engineer in charge, it is deemed necessary, the piles are to be shod with iron.

All piles injured, broken, driven out of line, or not in accordance with plan, shall be removed by the contractor. Piles shall be cut off at such a height and in such a manner that the timber platform can be framed thereon, as per plan, and at the grade established by the engineer in charge. 6 mooring-piles shall be driven 3 feet inside the front line of the platform, as shown by the plan, at points indicated by the engineer. They shall project 4 feet above the surface of the platform, and be firmly braced and secured as the engineer may direct. They shall be of white oak, at least 18 inches diameter at the top, and be driven to the same depth as the front piles of the platform.

The braces will be of white oak, not less than 5 inches diameter at the smaller end, and flattened where they bear against the piles and spur-shores.

All the timbers of the frame shall be of sound Southern pine, free from sap, shakes, and splits, and of the dimensions shown by the drawings.

The planks will be of spruce, sound, free from sap, shakes, splits, large or loose knots, and 4 inches thick ; of equal widths, not more than 12 inches, and shall break joint with each other. The length to be 14 feet, or some other multiple of 7.

Bolts are to be $1\frac{1}{4}''$ diameter, and the screw-threads are to be clean cut, and of suitable length for the nuts to come to a solid bearing.

The washers are to be $4''$ square and $\frac{1}{2}''$ thick.

The nuts are to be $2\frac{1}{4}''$ square and $1\frac{1}{4}''$ thick.

The planks are to be spiked with the best wrought-iron ship-spikes, $8''$ long.

All ironwork must be good wrought-iron, of such quality as the engineer will accept.

Treenails are to be of white oak, free from sap, and sound in every way, and $1\frac{1}{4}''$ in diameter.

All the work must be done in accordance with the plans and directions furnished by the engineer in charge, and must be done in a thorough, workmanlike manner, to the acceptance of the Land Commissioners and their engineer; and every opportunity must be given for inspection at all times

The Land Commissioners shall also have the right to reject any piles, timber, planks, or any portion of the ironwork, and to require the removal of any piece of wood or ironwork already in place which is unsatisfactory, and the substitution therefor of good material, and satisfactory to the Land Commissioners.

SPECIFICATIONS

FOR A FENDER FOR THE FACE OF THE HEAVY SEA-WALL WEST OF THE DOCK IN THE COMMONWEALTH'S FLATS AT SOUTH BOSTON.

The fender is to be built according to the plans on file at the chief engineer's office, on the South Boston Flats.

It consists of a row of piles driven close to the face of the wall, and strapped thereto, and a capsill framed on to the heads of the piles.

The piles are to be of oak, excluding black oak, sound, straight, and free from decay. They will be 35 feet long, and not less than .8 inches diameter at the smaller end, shod with iron, and driven close to the face of the wall, as per plan, and 6 feet apart. All piles broken, injured, driven out of position, or not in accordance with the plans, shall be removed by the contractor. Piles shall be cut off at such a height and in such a manner that the capsill can be framed thereon as per plan, and at the grade established by the engineer in charge. The piles shall be strapped to the wall, by iron straps of the size and shape shown on the plan. The ends of the straps will be fastened in drill-holes in the wall, as shown by the plan.

The iron to be of good quality wrought iron, acceptable to the engineer.

The capsill is to be framed on to the heads of the piles, and connected with the capsills of the platforms to be built at both ends of the wall. The treenails shall be of white oak, $1\frac{1}{4}''$ inches in diameter, sound, and free from decay or sap.

All the work must be done in accordance with the plans and directions furnished by the engineer in charge, and must be done in a thorough and workmanlike manner, to the acceptance of the Land Commissioners and their engineer; and every opportunity must be given at all times for inspection. The Land Commissioners shall have the right to reject any piles, timbers, or any portion of the ironwork, and to require the removal of any piece of wood or ironwork, already in place, which is unsatisfactory, and the substitution therefor of good material, and satisfactory to the Land Commissioners.

SPECIFICATIONS

FOR A FENDER FOR THE FACE OF THE HEAVY SEA-WALL EAST OF THE DOCK IN THE COMMONWEALTH'S FLATS AT SOUTH BOSTON.

The fender is to be built according to the plans on file at the chief engineer's office on the South Boston Flats. It consists of a row of piles driven close to the face of the wall, and strapped thereto, and a capsill framed on to the heads of the piles.

The piles are to be of oak, excluding black oak, sound, straight, and free from decay. They will be 50 feet long, and not less than 8 inches in diameter at the smaller end, shod with iron, and driven close to the face of the wall as per plan, and 6 feet apart. All piles broken, injured, driven out of position, or not in accordance with the plans, shall be removed by the contractor. Piles shall be cut off at such a height and in such a manner that the capsill can be framed thereon as per plan, and at the grade established by the engineer in charge.

The piles shall be strapped to the wall by iron straps of the size and shape shown on the plan. The ends of the straps will be fastened in drill-holes in the wall, as shown by the plan.

The iron is to be of good quality wrought iron, acceptable to the engineer.

The capsill is to be framed on to the heads of the piles, and connected with the capsills of the platforms to be built at both ends of the wall.

The treenails shall be of white oak, $1\frac{1}{4}''$ in diameter, sound, and free from decay or sap.

All work must be done in accordance with the plans and directions furnished by the engineer in charge, and must be done in a thorough and workmanlike manner, to the acceptance of the Land Commissioners and their engineer; and every opportunity must be given at all times for inspections.

The Land Commissioners shall have the right to reject any piles, timbers, or any portion of the ironwork, and to require the removal of any piece of wood or ironwork which is already in place, if it is unsatisfactory, and the substitution therefor of good material, and satisfactory to the Land Commissioners.

[Copy.]

PARK DEPARTMENT, No. 87 MILK ST.,
POST-OFFICE SQUARE, BOSTON, Dec. 6, 1878.

HORACE C. BACON, Esq., *Land Commissioner.*

Dear Sir, — In reply to your note of 3d inst , I beg to say, that we do not favor any encroachment into the Charles-river Basin beyond the 200 feet we have proposed for a public park, and we cannot therefore join your Board in asking that the harbor line be revised otherwise than as proposed by ourselves.

It has long been the general opinion, that these flats should not be covered by structures; and, should it be proper to take any part in a discussion in the premises, we should oppose such a revision of the line as would enable the Commonwealth to utilize any portion of its flats for building purposes.   In regard to compensation to the Commonwealth, our expectation has always been that the Commonwealth would gladly donate to the city of Boston the area as proposed by us, to be used solely as a public promenade; thus converting it from a nuisance, as at present, to a useful purpose.

I am unable to say how soon we shall be able to enter upon the improvement.

Very respectfully,

CHARLES H. DALTON, *Chairman.*

Commonwealth of Massachusetts.

HARBOR COMMISSIONERS' OFFICE, No. 8 PEMBERTON SQUARE,
BOSTON, Jan. 17, 1878.

To the Honorable Land Commissioners.

Dear Sirs, — The Harbor Commissioners are able to report the *filling* of the Twenty-five Acre Piece, South Boston Flats, under contracts with Rockport Granite Company and Messrs. Clapp and Ballou, completed. There remains some dredging being done to comply with requirements of their contracts, which is being deposited elsewhere; but there remains nothing which should prevent your Board entering at once into possession of the reclaimed territory, and we take pleasure in turning the same over to your care.

Very respectfully,

ALBERT MASON,
In behalf of Harbor Commission.

LAND COMMISSIONERS' OFFICE, STATE HOUSE,
BOSTON, Dec. 4, 1878.

D. WALDO LINCOLN, Esq., *President Boston & Albany Railroad.*

Dear Sir, — For the reason suggested to you in our conversation the other day, it seems very desirable that some further progress should be made towards a settlement of the account between the Commonwealth and your company.

The estimated amount of purchase by your company under contract of Dec. 8, 1869, was	$435,600
The estimate for land surrendered by your company (south of Eastern Avenue)	25,600
Which leaves estimated balance due from your company as cash, Oct. 1, 1876	$410,000
On April 8, 1878, you paid on account	330,000
Leaving	$80,000
To this amount add interest on $400,000, 18 months $36,900	
To this amount add interest on $80,000, 6 months . 2,400	
And you have for interest due	$39,300
To this add estimated balance of account	80,000
And you have	119,300

as the approximate balance of account due the State Oct. 1, 1878, beside any claim for damages through non-fulfilment of your contract. From this you claim an allowance of the several items enumerated in House Doc. No. 21, of 1878, p. 43, should be deducted. These amount to · . . . 66,724

This shows that	$52,576

or over $50,000, is now due to the Commonwealth without attempting to settle any of the points now at issue, and which are specifically enumerated on pp 55 and 56 of the document above referred to; and it is this sum of $50,000 which the Land Commissioners now desire your company to pay into the State Treasury.

And now we desire again to call your attention to point at issue No. 2 (p. 55, House Doc. 21 of 1858). The question of access to the Twenty-five Acre Lot has become a very serious one to the State. That lot was completed and was ready for occupancy nearly a year ago, but there was no way of getting to it, owing to the delay of your company in completing its part of the agreement of four parts; which prevents our now asking for the construction of Northern-avenue Bridge. Because of this inaccessibility we have been compelled to lease the property at a rent which is too low for what has cost the State so large a sum.   The lease made is for a very short term, because we hope that you will so hasten the completion of your sea-wall and filling as will enable the State at the earliest possible day to secure the construction of Northern-avenue Bridge.   With that avenue of communication opened, the land will be accessible and in demand.   Until it is opened, the full value of this land either for sale or lease cannot be secured.   The time for the opening of this avenue depends entirely upon your company, which, by its promptness or delay in the execution of its agreement with the State, can fix the length of time during which the State must continue to receive only a nominal rent for its property.   We should therefore fail in our duty if we refrained from calling your attention to the matter, and again asking that you will permit no further delay which can possibly be avoided.

We understand that your company has contracted for a portion of its filling and for the filling of Eastern Avenue, so that ere long this latter item of account can be adjusted.

We understand also that your company is prepared to release to the Commonwealth all the land south of Eastern Avenue, including the strip 40 feet in width heretofore reserved for roadbed, for tracks.   Our engineer, in connection with the city engineer and other parties in interest, is now about completing his survey of the land in South Boston.   When this is completed, and the line of Eastern Avenue is fixed by the city, it will be possible to determine your western boundary, the exact quantity of land included in your purchase of 1869, and the length of stone wall built by you in front of your land.   All these we hope to be able to arrange within thirty days, and afterwards the other points at issue can be considered.

Meanwhile the payment of the additional sum of $50,000 will be most acceptable, and will enable us to close our doings for the year with an acknowledgment of the payment by your company to the Commonwealth of an amount approximating somewhat nearly to the amount of your original purchase.

Very respectfully your ob't s'v't,

WILLARD P. PHILLIPS,
Chairman.

BOSTON & ALBANY RAILROAD COMPANY,
BOSTON, Dec. 14, 1878.

HON. WILLARD P. PHILLIPS, *Chairman of Board of Land Commissioners.*

Dear Sir, — Your communication dated Dec. 4 was received by me on the 7th inst., and I have the honor to reply with as little delay as possible. By the indenture of Dec. 8, 1869, the Commonwealth agreed to sell to the Boston & Albany Railroad Company a certain area of flats in South Boston, specifically defined therein by metes and bounds, but which was assumed to contain about 50 acres; and the railroad company

agreed to pay the Commonwealth therefor the sum of $435,600, which
is at the rate of 20 cents a foot for said 50 acres. The contract, however, provided that when the said area shall have been filled, the same
shall be surveyed, and the said price of $435,600 shall be diminished
or increased at the rate of 20 cents a foot, according as said area, exclusive of Northern and Eastern Avenue, and the extension of B Street, shall
be ess or more than 50 acres. The said area has not yet all been filled, nor
has it been surveyed, but there does not seem to be any good reason why
the survey should be dependent on the filling. The railroad company
have no means of determining for themselves the exact nor even the
approximate area contained within said defined limits. According to
the estimate furnished to the company by the engineer employed by the
Harbor Commissioners, the whole area to be conveyed to the said company by the Commonwealth, after deducting 128,000 feet south of Eastern Avenue which the railroad has surrendered as provided in the
supplementary contract, is 1,793,524 feet. Of this area 126,984 feet valued
at 50 cents a foot was taken in exchange for 317,460 feet at 20 cents a
foot. The whole area therefore, by this estimate, to be conveyed
to the railroad company, is equivalent to 1,986,000 feet. The Land
Commissioners, on the other hand, assume the quantity to be the
full amount of 50 acres less the 128,000 feet released. From this
area, when it shall have been surveyed, is to be deducted the area embraced within the limits of Northern Avenue, and the extension of B
Street. The company also claim credit, in the settlement, for certain
money paid out in fulfilment of its contract with the Commonwealth,
and for other money for work to be done for the Commonwealth for
which it is liable under existing contracts. These claims amount to the
sum of $66,724. On the 3d of April last, the railroad company paid to
the Commonwealth, in cash, the sum of $330,000, which was the amount
as near as it could be ascertained, exclusive of interest, which was
acknowledged to be due. I now understand that for the purpose of the
present approximate settlement, the Commissioners allow the credits
claimed by the railroad company, but they claim as now due from the
company the further sum of $52,576, of which $39,300 represents
interest, and $13,276 appears to be the difference in the price of the 50
acres of flats as assumed by the Commissioners, and the 1,986,000 feet
as estimated by the State engineers. Your letter informs me that the
engineers are now completing the survey of these flats; and I respectfully ask in behalf of the railroad company that payment should not be
required for the quantity of flats in dispute, until it is definitely determined by the surveys, if it is to be conveyed to and paid for by the railroad company. The remaining and large portion of the sum claimed is
for interest, viz., $39,300. The amount of interest, whatever it may be,
is subject to the same deductions as the principal on which the interest is
claimed. I respectfully submit to the Commissioners, that if the railroad company is not to pay for the area embraced within the limits of
Northern Avenue and the extension of B Street, as is specially stipulated in the contract, there is no reason why it should be called upon to
pay interest upon the price of that area, as if it was to be paid for. So,

also, of the $22,774 which the railroad company has actually paid in money for the heavy sea-wall, in strict fulfilment of the contract with the Commonwealth: I do not see why we should pay the State interest on that sum. The company has been paying or losing the interest on that sum ever since the money was expended. Deducting 2 years interest on the sum of $66,724, for which credit is claimed by the railroad company, amounting to $8,006, the sum claimed by the Commissioners will be reduced to $31,394.

In regard to this claim for interest and to the views of the railroad company in relation thereto, I again respectfully refer the Commissioners to the considerations presented to them in a previous communication. In reply to that communication the Commissioners stated that "they failed to find anywhere the power vested in them to permit them to make the allowance of interest which the railroad company claims; but, as soon as the items of the account between the Commonwealth and the company are agreed upon, it would be the duty of the Commissioners to notify the Governor and Council of our request, and that duty the Board would perform promptly." Are not the items of the account now substantially agreed upon, or sufficiently so for the purposes of the present settlement, and to authorize the reference to the Governor and Council as proposed? The company desire, and will avail themselves of an opportunity, to appear and be heard in explanation of their claim.

I am very respectfully yours,

(Signed)   D. WALDO LINCOLN,
                                              President.

HOUSE . . . . . No. 21.

Commonwealth of Massachusetts.

HOUSE OF REPRESENTATIVES, January 25, 1878.

The Committee on Public Lands, who were ordered to procure and report, for the use of the Legislature, copies of contracts between the Commonwealth and the Boston and Albany Railroad Company and the City of Boston, and all correspondence relating to the same, submit as their report the following communication from the Land Commissioners, and the documents annexed thereto.

For the Committee,

LEVI C. WADE.

Commonwealth of Massachusetts.

OFFICE OF THE LAND COMMISSIONERS,
STATE HOUSE, BOSTON, January 23, 1878.

To the Joint Standing Committee on Public Lands.

GENTLEMEN : — The Land Commissioners, in accordance with your request of yesterday, have the honor to enclose to you herein the following papers; viz.: —

1. Contract between Commonwealth and Boston and Albany Railroad Company, December 8, 1864.

2. Supplementary contract, same parties, June 24, 1873.

3. Indenture of four parts, June 24, 1873.

4. Contract with Messrs. Clapp & Ballou, and bond, September 29, 1873.

5. Contract with Messrs. Clapp & Ballou, and bond, June 13, 1875.

6. Vote of Boston and Albany Railroad Company, October 25, 1877.

7. Communication of Boston and Albany Railroad Company, November 1, 1877.

8. Reply of Land Commissioners, November 30, 1877.

9. Rejoinder of Boston and Albany Railroad Company, December 27, 1877.

10. Memorandum of points at issue, January 15, 1877.

11. Letter of Mayor of Boston, indorsing order of City Council, November 23, 1877.

In their first annual report, dated October 15, 1877, the Land Commissioners referred to matters connected with the contracts between the Commonwealth and the City of Boston, and the Boston and Albany Railroad Company, and stated that a supplementary report would be made should further legislation be found necessary.

Rec. March 28, 1904.

The order which has been adopted by the Legislature asks for copies of contracts, correspondence, &c., respecting the South Boston Flats, which the Land Commissioners would have submitted with their supplementary report, as soon as the negotiations with the city of Boston or the Boston and Albany Railroad Company should have reached the point requiring legislative action. And in submitting these papers now, in the unfinished state of the negotiations with the parties named, the Land Commissioners deem it necessary to make some statements and some explanations, so as to prevent any misunderstanding of the matters.

The first contract made by the Commonwealth with the Boston and Albany Railroad Company was in December, 1869, and is sent with this, as are also the contracts of June 24, 1873, with that company, and the indenture of four parts made on same day. All these contracts, as well as the subsequent contracts of 1874 and 1875 with Clapp & Ballou, and others, for the building of a sea-wall, and for the filling of the twenty-five-acre piece (so called), were made by the Board of Harbor Commissioners, acting for the Commonwealth, and duly approved by the Governor and Council. The Board of Harbor Commissioners continued to exercise full power over all these flats, and have exclusive charge of filling, &c., until May, 1875, when, by an Act of the Legislature, chapter 239, the flats in South Boston were placed in charge of the new Board of State Agents for the South Boston Flats, except as to certain matters, as specified in said Act, which were reserved to the Harbor Commissioners, and the agents were authorized to make new contracts for filling, &c., but no authority was given to them in regard to the contracts then existing for filling, &c. Consequently the Harbor Commissioners have continued to supervise the building of the seawall and the filling of the twenty-five-acre piece until the 17th of January, present, when they advised the Land Commissioners that the filling of the twenty-five-acre piece was completed, and turned it over to the Land Commissioners, who are now in charge of and have control over all the lands and flats of the Commonwealth in South Boston, except that all " contracts for improvement, sale, or use of said flats shall be first subject to the approval of the Board of Harbor Commissioners in regard to the lines upon the harbor, the method of construction of walls and piers, the maintaining of channels, and the taking of 'filling from the harbor of Boston."

In regard to the Boston and Albany matters, it will be noticed, that, under the supplementary contract of 1873, the flats purchased under the contract of 1869 were to have been filled on October 1, 1876, when the amount of $435,600, less certain specified deductions, should have been paid to the Commonwealth by said company. The State Treasurer has made two demands for this money, which caused a succession of interviews between the officers of that company and the Land Commissioners, and finally the correspondence herein enclosed. After the communication of the Boston and Albany Railroad Company, under date of 27th December, 1877, it was deemed best to have an interview with the committee of that company. This interview was had on 15th January, when the "points at issue," herein enclosed, were discussed, and another interview arranged for.

The order passed by the City Council of Boston, on November 12, 1877, in regard to the filling of B or C Street, has not been acted upon by the Land Commissioners, who have desired to settle the matters between the Commonwealth and the Boston and Albany Railroad Company, and then with that company to arrange with the city of Boston for the filling of the streets named, and for other matters provided for in the indenture of four parts.

The Land Commissioners desire to call your attention also to the provisions contained in the indenture of four parts, wherein the city of Boston agrees to locate and lay out Northern Avenue, and to build the Northern Avenue Bridge, so called, after the completion of the filling of the flats of the Commonwealth (now completed), the flats of the Boston and Albany Railroad Company, and the flats of the Boston Wharf Company. This bridge was to have been the avenue of communication between the twenty-five-acre lot, so called, and the city proper. But as the Boston and Albany Railroad Company has not yet completed its filling, the city of Boston may decline to build its bridge at the present time, or until the filling agreed to be done by the Boston and Albany Railroad Company shall have been completed. As yet, that company has done very little filling, so that the Commonwealth has now a large tract of land, of great cost, which cannot be used until some communication with it is secured. To this matter the attention of the Boston and Albany Railroad Company has been called, and at the next interview it is expected that that company will make some suggestions in regard thereto. To the Land Commissioners it seems that the building of the bridge at Northern Avenue may depend upon the completion, by the Boston and Albany Railroad Company, of its filling upon the flats purchased in 1869; so that, if that company shall not complete its filling without delay, it may be necessary for the Commonwealth to enforce the provisions of the contract with the Boston and Albany Railroad Company, which permits the Commonwealth to complete the contract at the expense of the Boston and Albany Railroad Company, as the only way to secure a communication between the city proper and the lands of the Commonwealth, which have cost so much money.

The Land Commissioners regret that, in the present state of the negotiations with the Boston and Albany Railroad Company, it has been necessary to submit the correspondence with that company in its present unfinished state, as they had hoped and expected before long to have advised of a settlement with that company; and they still expect to be able to make such settlement.

There are other matters referred to in the Land Commissioners' Report of October 15, 1877, — the claim of Mrs. Cairns, and the unpurchased three-eightieths of the " Fan-Piece," so called, which still remain unsettled, and may require legislation. And there are other matters connected with the dock in the twenty-five-acre piece, and the arrangements necessary for filling B or C Street, if it is found imperative upon the Commonwealth to do that work, which will require legislative action.

Very respectfully, your obedient servant,

WILLARD P. PHILLIPS,
Chairman of the Land Commissioners.

Agreement between the Commonwealth of Massachusetts and the Boston and Albany Railroad Company.

Whereas, under an Act entitled "An Act authorizing the extension of the Boston and Albany Railroad to deep water at South Boston, and for other purposes," being chapter 461 of the Acts of the year 1869, the Boston and Albany Railroad Company desire to purchase a parcel of flats, in South Boston, of the Commonwealth of Massachusetts :

Now, therefore, the following Articles of Agreement, made this eighth day of December, A.D. eighteen hundred and sixty-nine, by and between the Commonwealth of Massachusetts, party of the first part, acting by its Board of Harbor Commissioners, and the Boston and Albany Railroad Company, a corporation organized under the laws of said Commonwealth, party of the second part, *Witness :*

That, in consideration of the covenants and agreements hereinafter made by the said party of the second part, the party of the first part hereby covenants and agrees with the said party of the second part, that it will, in six years from the first day of October, A.D. 1869, convey to said party of the second part, by a good and sufficient warranty deed, a certain parcel of flats situated in that part of Boston known as South Boston, and being a portion of the flats known as the South Boston flats, bounded and described as follows : Beginning at the north-westerly corner of the same on the exterior line, as shown on the plan annexed to the second annual report of the Board of Harbor Commissioners, and defined in said report, which point is also the north-easterly corner of the parcel of flats conveyed by the said Commonwealth to Peter Harvey, James S. Whitney and Henry B. Groves, trustees for the Boston, Hartford and Erie Railroad Company, by deed dated July 21, A.D. 1869, and recorded with Suffolk County Deeds in Lib. 970, Fol. 15, and is marked Y, on the plan hereto annexed marked A, and running south-westerly along the easterly line of land of said Harvey, Whitney and Groves, trustees as aforesaid, to a point on said plan marked L, in the Commissioners' line A, established by chapter 385 of the Acts of the year 1853, distant ten hundred and ninety-three feet easterly from the Commissioners' line on the easterly side of Fort Point Channel, established by chapter 35 of the Acts of the year 1840; thence running easterly along said Commissioners' line A, one hundred and fifty-six and a half feet to the point on said plan marked M; thence running south-westerly along the land of said Harvey, Whitney and Groves, trustees, parallel to said Commissioners' line on the easterly side of said Fort Point Channel six hundred and eighty-five feet to a point marked N, on the plan hereto annexed, marked A; thence running south-easterly at right angles to the last described line seven hundred and fourteen feet to a point marked O, on said plan A; thence running north-easterly to a point marked S, on said plan A, in said exterior line, as shown on the plan annexed to the second annual report of the Harbor Commissioners, eight hundred and seventy-eight feet easterly from the point of beginning; thence westerly eight hundred and seventy-eight feet to the point of beginning: *provided, however*, that said party of the first part shall not be bound to make such conveyance until said parcel of flats shall have been occupied and improved by the filling of the same, and the construction on the same of walls and bulkheads and otherwise, as hereinafter covenanted and agreed by said party of the second part.

Said covenant and agreement are, and said conveyance when made shall be, upon the following reservations and restrictions: —

First. Said Commonwealth reserves in said territory the right by its Harbor Commissioners, subject to the approval of the governor and council, to locate upon, over and across the said territory Northern Avenue, seventy-five feet in width, and Eastern Avenue, sixty-six feet in width, and to locate an extension or continuation of B Street as far as to its intersection with said Northern Avenue, substantially as said avenues and street are shown on said plan marked A, and to appropriate and devote the territory embraced within the limits of said avenues and street, when so located, to all the uses and purposes of public street and highways without compensation to said party of the second part or their successors for the territory appropriated or the filling of the same.

Second. Any and all plans for the drainage of said parcel of flats when filled shall be submitted, before commencing the work for such drainage, to the Board of Harbor Commissioners, and shall be subject to their approval and the approval of the governor and council.

And said party of the second part, in consideration of the covenants and agreements of said party of the first part, hereby covenants and agrees with said party of the first part, that it will pay to said party of the first part or its assigns, in three years from the first day of October, A.D. 1869, four hundred and thirty-five thousand six hundred dollars, ($435,600,) either in cash or the bonds of said party of the second part, payable in twenty years from the first day of October, A.D. 1872, with interest thereon at the rate of six per centum per annum, payable semi-annually.

And said party of the second part, for the consideration aforesaid, further covenants and agrees with said party of the first part, that it will build within six years from said first day of October, A.D. 1869, unless, for good cause shown, the Harbor Commissioners, with the consent of the governor and council, shall extend said time, a sea-wall, commencing at a point in the north-westerly boundary line of said parcel of flats hereinbefore bounded. and described, distant southerly one foot from the said exterior line, as the same is laid down on the plan annexed to the second annual report of the Board of Harbor Commissioners, and extending south-easterly parallel to said exterior line to the easterly boundary line of said parcel of flats, and unite said wall with the sea-wall built on a line one foot within said exterior line, and on the said adjoining westerly parcel of flats conveyed by the Commonwealth to said Harvey, Whitney and Groves, trustees, so that both walls shall form a continuous and uniform structure. The said sea-wall shall be built by said party of the second part on said line parallel to said exterior line, and one foot within the same, as shown by the red line on the said plan hereto annexed marked A, and in such location as shall be marked out by the engineer of the Board of Harbor Commissioners previously to the commencement of the work of building the same by the party of the second part; and said party of the second part shall preserve the location of said line by driving piles to mark the location of the wall permanently. Such sea-wall shall be built in accordance with the plan marked B, hereto annexed:

Provided, however, that in the line of said wall an opening, or openings, may be left for a dock, or docks, of such width, dimensions, and construction as the Harbor Commissioners shall approve, which opening or openings shall be filled temporarily by bulkheads constructed in such manner as the Harbor Commissioners may prescribe.

The trench for this sea-wall shall be excavated under the direction and to the satisfaction of the Board of Harbor Commissioners, from twenty-three to twenty-five feet in width at the bottom, which shall be as nearly as practicable a level surface. The depth of the trench shall be at least twenty-three feet below mean low water, and always to hard bottom.

The wall to the height of one foot below low water shall be built in quarry-face dimension stone of granite, laid in courses of two feet rise each, by the aid of submarine divers. The courses shall be laid alternately entirely with headers and stretchers, the bottom, or first course, being headers. Each stone shall be at least four feet and not more than ten feet long, at least eighteen inches wide, and exactly two feet rise. The wall shall be compactly laid in a substantial and workmanlike manner, with fair and close outer face. Stones shall be laid so as to break joints everywhere, with good and sufficient bearing upon the beds without pinners. The front face of the wall shall have a batter of four inches to the foot, and the rear of the wall shall be perpendicular. The base of the wall shall be eighteen feet, the height of the wall to one foot below mean low water twenty-two feet, and the thickness of the wall at this level eleven feet four inches. The wall from one foot below mean low water to the top of the coping stones, or grade sixteen, shall be laid with dimension stones in cement. The courses shall be laid with headers and stretchers, and have two feet rise, with the exception of the coping course, which shall have a rise of three feet, and be entirely of headers. The stretchers shall be at least four feet long, and the headers shall not be less than five feet long from the face inwardly. The spaces, however, back of the stretchers, and between the headers, may be filled with quarry stones of large dimensions, laid compactly in cement, so as to form solid masonry. The front batter of the face shall be four inches to the foot. The base of this wall shall be nine feet eight inches, the height seventeen feet, and the thickness at the top of the wall five feet. The ends of all the sections of the wall shall be faced up in the manner above required.

And said party of the second part may, along the line of sea-wall to be built by it, but within the exterior line shown on the plan annexed to the second annual report of the Harbor Commissioners, construct, maintain, and use for wharf purposes, a suitable platform, not to exceed fourteen feet in width outside of the top of such sea-wall.

And said party of the second part, for the considerations aforesaid, further covenants and agrees with said party of the first part, that it will within six years from the first day of October, A.D. 1869, unless, for good cause shown, the Harbor Commissioners, with the consent of the governor and council, shall extend said

time, fill all of the said parcel of lands and flats hereinbefore
bounded and described in the manner following:

The filling shall be to grade thirteen with dredged material, and
said material shall be dredged from the trench to be made for the
sea-wall hereinbefore described, and from the area shaded red as
set forth on the plan annexed to the second annual report of the
Harbor Commissioners, and shall be deposited in such localities as
may be designated by the Board of Harbor Commissioners, provided that material may be taken from other portions of the harbor of Boston for such filling, with the assent of the Board of
Harbor Commissioners and the governor and council; and upon the
request of said Board, and governor and council, shall be so taken,
after the area shaded red shall have been dredged out to the required
depth. The area shaded red, and all other portions of Boston Harbor where dredging shall be authorized for filling as aforesaid, shall
be dredged to such depth and in such sections as may be directed
by the Harbor Commissioners, but no portion of the same is to be
dredged to more than twenty-three feet below mean low water.
But said party of the second part shall, whenever required by the
Board of Harbor Commissioners, fill on any portion of the westerly
line of said parcel of flats, simultaneously with the progress of or
after the filling or other occupation there on the easterly line of the
westerly-adjoining flats, conveyed by said Commonwealth and the
Boston Wharf Company to said Harvey, Whitney and Groves.
The sections in progress of filling shall be wholly or partially enclosed by said sea-wall and by temporary bulkheads to the satisfaction of the Board of Harbor Commissioners. The dredged material must be deposited to grade thirteen; and, so soon thereafter
as is practicable, the territory thus filled must be raised to grade sixteen by filling with clean gravel or other material, to the satisfaction
of the Harbor Commissioners and the governor and council; but
nothing herein contained shall be construed to require said Boston
and Albany Railroad Company to remove any ledge of rock that
may be found in dredging outside the limits of the flats to be conveyed to said company as aforesaid.

And said party of the second part, for the considerations aforesaid, hereby covenants and agrees with the party of the first part
that it will fill up as aforesaid that portion of the flats to be conveyed to said party of the second part upon which the party of
the first part shall locate Northern and Eastern Avenues, and the
extension or continuation of B Street as herein provided, whenever
required by the Board of Harbor Commissioners with the assent
of the governor and council; and that whenever the Commonwealth

by its Harbor Commissioners, or otherwise, shall authorize the filling of the flats on the easterly line of said parcel hereinbefore described, and the work of such filling shall begin, the said party of the second part will fill the flats on such easterly line so far and at such time as the Harbor Commissioners may prescribe for the protection of the filling of the adjoining territory.

It is further agreed between the parties hereto, that, when said territory shall have been filled as herein provided, the same shall be surveyed by the engineer of the Board of Harbor Commissioners, and said price of four hundred and thirty-five thousand six hundred dollars to be paid for said flats as herein provided shall be increased or diminished at the rate of twenty cents per square foot, according as the number of feet, exclusive of Northern and Eastern Avenues and the extension of B Street over said territory, shall be found more or less than fifty acres; and the amount so found due the party of the first part, if any, shall be paid by the party of the second part in cash, with interest, if any shall have accrued; or in case the price shall be found less than four hundred and thirty-five thousand six hundred dollars, then such price shall be reduced to that extent, or the same and such interest as shall have been paid thereon shall be refunded to said party of the second part, or credited as a partial payment of its bonds, as the case may require.

And said party of the first part hereby authorizes the said party of the second part to enter upon said parcel of flats hereinbefore bounded and described, and hold possession of and use the same when filled, so long as it shall keep and perform its said covenants and agreements herein contained, and no longer; but in case of default therein on the part of said party of the second part, the said party of the first part shall have authority by its Board of Harbor Commissioners, subject to the approval of the governor and council, forthwith to enter upon said land or flats, and resume possession of the same, and do and perform, at the expense of said party of the second part, every thing which said party of the second part is bound hereby to do and perform upon and in relation to said land or flats; and said party of the second part hereby agrees to pay to said party of the first part, upon the conveyance of said flats, in addition to the price aforesaid, ascertained in the manner aforesaid, any and all expenses which the said party of the first part shall so incur.

In testimony whereof, the said Commonwealth of Massachusetts has hereunto fixed its seal by the hands of its Harbor Commissioners, who have subscribed their names hereto, and the said Boston and Albany Railroad Company has hereunto set its corporate seal by the hand of its president, thereunto duly authorized by the vote of the directors of said company, a copy of which is hereto annexed.

COMMONWEALTH OF MASSACHUSETTS, [SEAL.]

By JOSIAH QUINCY,
S. E. SEWALL,
DARWIN E. WARE,
F. W. LINCOLN, Jr.,
J. N. MARSHALL,
Harbor Commissioners.

THE BOSTON AND ALBANY R. R. CO.,
By C. W. CHAPIN, *President.* [SEAL.]

COMMONWEALTH OF MASSACHUSETTS.

SUFFOLK, ss. Then personally appeared C. W. Chapin, president of the Boston and Albany Railroad Company, and acknowledged the above to be the free act and deed of the said corporation. Before me,

MOSES KIMBALL, *Justice of the Peace.*

BOSTON AND ALBANY RAILROAD COMPANY.

At a meeting of the Board of Directors in Boston, December 8, 1869, the contract between the Boston and Albany Railroad Company, and the Commonwealth of Massachusetts through the Harbor Commissioners, for the purchase and filling of fifty acres of land of the South Boston Flats, having been read and considered, it was

Voted, That the president be and he is hereby authorized to execute the same for and on behalf of this corporation.

A true copy from the Record.

Attest:　　　　J. A. RUMRILL, *Clerk.*

COUNCIL CHAMBER, BOSTON, December 8, 1869. The foregoing contract is this day approved by the Governor and Council.

OLIVER WARNER, *Secretary of the Commonwealth.*

Indenture of Four Parts, between the Common-. wealth, the Boston and Albany Railroad Company, the Boston Wharf Company, and the City of Boston.

This Indenture, made this twenty-fourth day of June, eighteen hundred aud seventy-three, by and between the Commonwealth of Massachusetts, acting by its Board of Harbor Commissioners, subject to the approval of the governor and council, of the first part, the Boston and Albany Railroad Company, a corporation established under the laws of said Commonwealth, of the second part; the Boston Wharf Company, a corporation also established, under said laws, of the third part, and the City of Boston of the fourth part, *Witnesseth:*

That the said party of the first part, in consideration of the obligations of the party of the fourth part herein contained, hereby covenants and agrees with said party of the fourth part, that before the first day of October, A.D. 1876, it will fill with solid filling, to the grade of sixteen feet above mean low water, the parcel of flats belonging to the said party of the first part, situated at the junction of the Main Channel and Fort Point Channel, in Boston Harbor, and bounded south-west by the flats of the Boston Wharf Company, and south-east by the flats sold by the Commonwealth to the Boston and Albany Railroad Company, and described in the agreement between said Commonwealth and said Boston and Albany Railroad Company, dated December 8, A.D. 1869, and appended to the Fourth Annual Report of the Harbor Commissioners to the Legislature, and in an agreement of even date with these presents modifying said agreement of said 8th of December; and will, before said first day of October, build a sea-wall around the margin of said parcel of flats upon said Main and Fort Point Channels; excepting, however, from this covenant and agreement so much of said flats as shall be reserved for docks.

And the said party of the second part, in consideration of the obligations of the party of the fourth part herein contained, hereby covenants and agrees with the said party of the fourth part, that before the first day of October, A.D. 1876, it will fill with solid filling, to the grade of sixteen feet above mean low water, the flats described in said agreements, and sold by said Commonweath to said Boston and Albany Railroad Company; and will, before said first day of October, build a sea-wall on the north-east side of said parcel of flats; excepting, however, from this covenant and agreement such portion of the said flats as shall be reserved for docks, and the space required for the natural- slope of the filling on the south-east and south-west boundary lines of said flats.

And said party of the third part, in consideration of the obligations of said party of the fourth part herein contained, hereby covenants and agrees with said party of the fourth part, that it will, in eighteen months from the date of these presents, fill to said grade sixteen, with solid filling, its flats lying north-east of Commissioners' line A, and south-east of the Commissioners' line on the south-east side of Fort Point Channel, as said party of the third part now is or shall hereafter be authorized to fill the same; and will, within the said eighteen months, build a sea-wall on the south-west side of said flats; excepting, however, from this covenant and agreement such portion of said flats as shall be reserved for docks.

And the said party of the fourth part, in consideration of the foregoing obligations of said parties of the first, second and third parts, hereby covenants and agrees with each of said parties of the first, second and third parts, its successors and assigns, that it will, after the walls and solid filling the said parties of the first and second parts have hereinbefore agreed to build and to do have been completed, and the flats to be filled by said party of the second part have been conveyed by said party of the first part to said party of the second part, and within twelve months after the request of the Board of Harbor Commissioners, approved by the governor and council, build a bridge for public travel over Fort Point Channel in extension of Northern Avenue, substantially as said avenue is located on the plan for the occupation of flats owned by the Commonwealth in Boston Harbor, annexed to the Sixth Annual Report of said Harbor Commissioners to the Legislature.

And said party of the fourth part further covenants and agrees with each of said parties, that it will, within eighteen months from the date of these presents, build a bridge for public travel across Fort Point Channel in extension of Eastern Avenue, and extend Eastern Avenue to some existing street on the north-westerly side of Fort Point Channel, substantially as said avenue is located on said plan annexed to said Sixth Annual Report of the Harbor Commissioners, but at such a distance from the bridge of the Boston, Hartford and Erie Railroad, that the draws in both bridges may be operated without interference with one another, and be convenient for the passage of vessels, or in such manner under section six of chapter three hundred and twenty-six of the Acts of the year eighteen hundred and sixty-eight that the extension of said avenue may form a convenient connection with Congress Street. But said party of the fourth part shall not be obliged by this indenture to build said bridges and extend said avenue at a greater cost than the estimate of the city engineer, dated June 15, 1872, appended to the report of a joint special committee of the city council on the memorial of the Harbor Commissioners, asking the co-operation of the city in certain respects in the occupation of the South Boston Flats ; and said party of the fourth part hereby agrees forthwith to locate said Eastern Avenue under the provisions of said sixth section of said three hundred and twenty-sixth chapter of the Acts of the year eighteen hundred and sixty-eight.

It is further agreed between said party of the first part and said party of the fourth part, that the style of the draws in said bridges to be built by said party of the fourth part, and that the piling for said bridges and draws, shall be determined by the board of aldermen of said city of Boston and said Harbor Commissioners, provided that the width of the passage-ways for vessels shall not be less than thirty-six feet, and that the grade of said bridges shall be satisfactory to the surveyors of highways of said city.

And it is further agreed between said parties of the first and fourth parts, that said party of the first part shall assume and pay into the compensation fund for Boston Harbor whatever shall be assessed under the fourth section of chapter one hundred and forty-nine of the Acts of the year 1866, as compensation for tide-water displaced by the said party of the fourth part in building said bridges and extending said avenues, except the amount, not exceeding thirty-five hundred dollars, which shall be assessed on account of the extension of said Eastern Avenue, which amount the said party of the third part hereby agrees with said party of the first part to assume, and pay into the treasury of the Commonwealth.

And said party of the fourth part, for the consideration aforesaid, hereby covenants and agrees with said party of the first part, that in case it shall fail to build said bridges and extend said avenues, or either of them, to some existing street on the north-westerly side of Fort Point Channel, the said party of the first part may build said bridges and extend said avenues for and on account of said party of the fourth part ; and that it, the said party of the fourth part, will pay to said party of the first part all reasonable expenses, not exceeding said estimate of the city engineer, which the party of the first part shall incur in building said bridges and extending said avenues as aforesaid, or either of them.

And said parties of the first, second, and third parts hereby further covenant and agree, each for itself, with said party of the fourth part, that they will respectively fill to the grade of sixteen feet above mean low water so much of their several parcels of land or flats between Fort Point Channel and the south-easterly line of said flats sold by the Commonwealth to the Boston and Albany Railroad Company as lie within the limits of said Northern and Eastern Avenue, as said avenues shall be defined and located under this indenture; and, in addition, that they will fill said avenues, on their respective parcels, in such a manner as to form a proper and convenient grade, satisfactory to the surveyors of highways for said city, with the extensions of said avenues, and the bridges which said party of the fourth part shall construct as herein provided, so soon as said extensions of said avenues and said bridges shall respectively be completed.

And said parties of the first, second, and third parts further agree, each for itself, with said party of the fourth part, that said party of the fourth part may lay out as public streets, without incurring any liability for land damages for so doing, said Northern Avenue not more than one hundred feet wide, Eastern Avenue not more than seventy-five feet wide (the exact width of said avenues to be determined by the party of the first part, unless determined by the said party of the fourth part, within one year after said territory is filled), and the extension of B Street seventy-five feet wide on the north-easterly side of Eastern Avenue, over the said respective parcels of the said parties of the first, second, and third parts lying between Fort Point Channel and the south-easterly boundary line of said flats sold by the Commonwealth to said Boston and Albany Railroad Company, as said avenues and the extension of B Street are shown on said plan of occupation, or as the same shall be located under this indenture.

And said parties of the first, second, and third parts further agree, that when said avenues and said extension of B Street within said limits shall have been filled and laid out as herein provided, they will each convey to said party of the fourth part the fee of their said respective parcels within the limits of said avenues, and said extension of B Street; but said party of the second part hereby reserves the right in its said parcel, and in such conveyance may reserve the right, to lay its tracks at grade across Eastern Avenue, the extension of B Street north-easterly of Eastern Avenue, and across Northern Avenue, and to lay its tracks, not exceeding two, at grade along said Northern Avenue and the said extension of B Street north-easterly of Eastern

Avenue, as authorized by the fourth section of chapter four hundred and sixty-one of the Acts of the year eighteen hundred and sixty-nine ; the location of said tracks along said extension of B Street and Northern Avenue to be determined by said party of the second part, with the assent and approval of the surveyors of highways of said city of Boston.

And said parties of the first, second, and third parts further agree, each for itself, with said party of the fourth part, that said party of the fourth part may build main sewers, and such other sewers as the board of health of the city of Boston may deem necessary for the proper drainage of the territory to be filled by said parties of the first, second, and third parts, as herein described, and any territory abutting thereon or connected therewith, and may use any street, passage-way or dock for the purpose of such sewers or drains, and discharge the contents thereof in said docks, or in front of said sea-walls, as the board of health of said city may direct ; and said party of the fourth part may assess a just and equitable portion of the expense thereof upon the lots in said territory to be filled by said parties of the first, second, and third parts, which shall be benefited thereby ; said assessment to be laid according to the rules established for the city sewers, and according to the laws of the Commonwealth relating thereto at the time such drains shall be built ; the amount of such assessments to be paid by the owners of such lots when the same shall be filled up as aforesaid and require drains, and in no case before.

And said party of the first part further covenants and agrees with said party of the fourth part, that as the other territory of the South Boston flats belonging to said party of the first part, within the limits of the first section of said South Boston flats, as shown on said plan of occupation appended to said Sixth Annual Report, including the extension of L Street, shall be filled to grade, the said party of the first part will provide that Northern Avenue and Eastern Avenue, as shown on said plan, or as the same may be located under this indenture, the extensions of C, D, E, F, and K Streets to Eastern Avenue, the extension of L Street as shown on said plan, and the extension of B Street below the hundred-rod line, as shown on said plan, shall, so far as such avenues and extensions are within the said territory, and as fast as the portions of the territory bordering on said avenues and extensions are filled, also be filled to the grade of sixteen feet above mean low water ; and further, that said party of the fourth part may within the said territory lay out the same when filled as pub-

3

lic streets, without incurring any land damages for so doing, and
that, when so laid out as public streets, said party of the fourth
part shall have a conveyance of the said territory within the limits
of said avenues and the said extension of streets.

And the said party of the first part, for the considerations
aforesaid, further covenants and agrees with said party of the
fourth part, that within one year after the filling to be done by the
parties of the first, second, and third parts has been completed as
herein provided, it, the said party of the first part, will build, so as
to connect with Eastern Avenue, the extension from First Street,
of B Street or C Street, as the Harbor Commissioners may elect,
and that whichever of said streets said Commissioners may elect to
build shall be filled in such a manner as to form a proper and convenient grade satisfactory to the surveyors of highways of said
city of Boston ; and in case said Commissioners shall elect to build
C Street, that said party of the first part will build Eastern Avenue,
as hereinbefore provided, out to the extension of said C Street,
the said party of the fourth part hereby authorizing said party of
the first part to build said extension of B and C Streets as herein
provided.

And the said parties of the first and third parts further agree,
each for itself, with said party of the fourth part, that said party
of the fourth part may, within one year, lay out an avenue in
extension of Mount Washington Avenue south-eastwardly from
Granite Street over any flats of said parties now filled, and over
any other portions of the flats of said parties within the limits of
such extension, within one year after such portion is filled to grade
sixteen, without incurring any liability for land or grade damages
for so doing ; and that when so laid out they will respectively
convey to said party of the fourth part said territory within the
limits of the said avenue where the same is extended over their
lands.

And said parties of the first, second, and third parts, for the
considerations aforesaid, hereby, each for itself, covenants and
agrees with said party of the fourth part, that the party of the
fourth part shall be subjected to no grade or other damages for any
land taken of either of said parties, or any injury done to land of
either of said parties, on the south-east side of Fort Point Channel,
in performing its obligations under this indenture.

And said party of the third part, in consideration of the obligations of said party of the first part herein contained, hereby covenants and agrees with said party of the first part, that it will fill
its territory hereinbefore described as fast as the said party of

the first part shall fill its territory on the division line of their respective parcels, so that it will not be necessary to have a bulkhead or barrier on such division line to retain the filling of said party of the first part ; and that if said party of the third part shall not fill its said territory as fast as said party of the first part fills its territory on such line, so that a barrier or bulkhead as aforesaid becomes necessary, said party of the first part may build, at the expense of said party of the third part, such a bulkhead or barrier along such division line as may be necessary to retain the filling as aforesaid ; and whenever said party of the first part shall begin at said division line to build the sea-wall which it has hereinbefore agreed to build, the said party of the third part hereby agrees to begin at said line to build the sea-wall which it has herein agreed to build, and that it will prosecute the building of the same with vigor to its completion ; that it will, within eighteen months from the date of these presents, fill to grade sixteen its said territory, and will, after said Eastern Avenue has been located, and the building of the bridge therefor commenced, dredge the flats lying in the section of Fort Point Channel opposite its said territory uniformly to the thread of said channel, to the depth of twelve feet at mean low water ; and in case said party of the third part shall fail to begin or to prosecute the construction of said sea-wall, or to fill its said territory as herein provided, the said company hereby agrees that said Commonwealth may enter upon said territory, and build so much of said sea-wall, and do so much of said filling, as it shall see fit, at the expense of said party of the third part ; and said party of the third part hereby agrees to pay to said party of the first part all the reasonable expenses it shall incur in building said sea-wall, and in filling as aforesaid, on the territory of said party of the third part.

And said party of the third part hereby further covenants and agrees with said party of the first part, that the said party of the first part and its assigns shall have, at convenient places to be designated by said party of the third part, a right of way from the track of the New York and New England Railroad across the territory of said party of the third part, for the purpose of filling said adjoining territory of said party of the first part ; and that said party of the first part shall have the right to lay railroad tracks on the same, for the transportation in cars of material to be used in the work of filling said territory of the party of the first part ; but such right of way shall not continue after the first day of October, A.D. 1876. If said party of the third part shall not have filled its territory to grade sixteen before the first day of August, A.D. 1875,

so as to furnish a convenient right of way to the said territory of the
party of the first part, the said party of the first part shall have the
right to enter upon said territory of said party of the third part,
and fill, at the expense of said party of the third part, so much of
the same as may be required to furnish a convenient right of way
to said territory of the party of the first part, for the purpose of
transporting material as aforesaid to, and filling with such material,
said territory ; and said party of the third part hereby agrees to
pay to said party of the first part all the reasonable expenses it
shall incur in so filling such portion of the territory of said party
of the third part.

And said party of the third part hereby further covenants and
agrees, that, together with said party of the second part, if it shall
hereafter so agree, or otherwise, it will lay out a street for public
use in some convenient location, to be determined by said party of
the third part, not less than fifty feet in width, extending from
Eastern Avenue north-easterly to the north-easterly line of the territory of said party of the third part, within one year from the
completion of the filling of the territory of said party of the first
part, as hereinbefore agreed by said party of the first part ; provided that said party of the third part shall not before said time
have sold, for railroad purposes, its territory north-east of said
Eastern Avenue, or such part thereof as to make it inconvenient
for the railroad using said territory that said street should be laid
out ; and provided, also, that said party of the fourth part shall
lay out and extend said Eastern Avenue, or take land for said purpose, or take some other decisive action to extend said avenue, as
hereinbefore agreed by said party of the fourth part, within six
months from the date of these presents.

In testimony whereof, on the day and year first above written,
the said Commonwealth has caused its corporate seal to be hereto
affixed, and these presents to be signed, acknowledged and delivered in its name and behalf, by Josiah Quincy, Darwin E. Ware,
Frederic W. Lincoln, Joshua N. Marshall, and William T. Grammer, its Harbor Commissioners, and the same to be approved by
its governor and executive council ; and the said Boston and
Albany Railroad Company has caused its corporate seal to be hereto affixed, and these presents to be signed, acknowledged and delivered, in its name and behalf, by Chester W. Chapin, its president, thereunto duly authorized ; and the said Boston Wharf
Company has caused its corporate seal to be hereto affixed, and
these presents to be signed, acknowledged and delivered, in its
name and behalf, by Jacob Sleeper, its president, thereunto duly

authorized; and the said City of Boston has caused its corporate seal to be hereto affixed, and these presents to be signed, acknowledged and delivered, in its name and behalf, by Henry L. Pierce, its mayor, thereunto duly authorized by said city.

Signed sealed and delivered in presence of
HENRY L. WHITING.   [SEAL.]

COMMONWEALTH OF MASSACHUSETTS,

By JOSIAH QUINCY,
DARWIN E. WARE,
F. W. LINCOLN,
J. N. MARSHALL,
W. T. GRAMMER,
Harbor Commissioners.

BOSTON AND ALBANY RAILROAD CO.,
By C. W. CHAPIN, *President.*   [SEAL.]

BOSTON WHARF CO.,
By JACOB SLEEPER, *President.*   [SEAL.]

CITY OF BOSTON,
By HENRY L. PIERCE, *Mayor.*   [SEAL.]

COMMONWEALTH OF MASSACHUSETTS.

IN COUNCIL, July 15, 1873.
Approved: OLIVER WARNER, *Secretary.*

AGREEMENT BETWEEN THE COMMONWEALTH AND THE BOSTON AND
ALBANY RAILROAD COMPANY.

WHEREAS, by articles of agreement, dated December 8, A.D. 1869, made by and between the Commonwealth of Massachusetts, acting by its Board of Harbor Commissioners with the approval of the governor and council, and the Boston and Albany Railroad Company, a corporation organized under the laws of said Commonwealth, said Commonwealth agreed to sell, and said Company agreed to buy, a parcel of flats in Boston Harbor, upon certain terms set forth in said agreement, and said Company therein agreed to improve said flats by building a sea-wall upon them, and fill them according to the terms of said agreement; and whereas delays have occurred in the improvement of the flats lying north-westerly of those sold to said Company not anticipated when said agreement was made between said Company and the Commonwealth, which have tended to delay the improvement by said Company of the flats so purchased by it; and whereas, in arranging with the city of Boston the terms on which said Company might use its territory so purchased for railroad purposes consistently with the maintenance in the same locality of highways safe and convenient for travel, it has been found convenient that said Company should surrender to the Commonwealth so much of the flats purchased of the Commonwealth as lie south-west of the south-westerly line of Eastern Avenue as it shall be located over said territory, and should take of the Commonwealth, in place of the area surrendered, other flats; and whereas other modifications of said agreement have become expedient: Now, THEREFORE, the said Commonwealth, acting by its Board of Harbor Commissioners, subject to the approval of the governor and council, in consideration of the agreements herein contained of said Company, and the execution by said Company of an indenture of four parts, of even date with these presents, between said Commonwealth, said Boston and Albany Railroad Company, the Boston Wharf Company, and the City of Boston, hereby agrees to extend, and does extend, the time of the payment of the purchase-money stipulated in said agreement of said December 8, and the time for doing such work in relation to said territory as was required by said agreement to be done by the first day of October, A.D. 1875, to the first day of October A.D. 1876; and said Commonwealth hereby releases the said Company from all claim for interest on said purchase-money heretofore accrued, and agrees that no interest shall accrue on said purchase-money for any period prior to said last-mentioned date.

Said Commonwealth and said Company hereby release each the other from all its obligations in said agreement contained, in relation to so much of the parcel of flats described in said agreement as lies south-west of the south-westerly line of Eastern Avenue, as the same shall be laid out under the said indenture of four parts; and said Company hereby surrenders to said Commonwealth such portion of said flats described in said agreement of said 8th of December, free and discharged from the operation of the same, except such portion of said flats as is to be conveyed to said Company, as hereinafter provided, for a road-bed for its tracks; and in place of, and as an equivalent for, such flats so surrendered, the said Commonwealth hereby agrees with said Company to convey to it of the area of flats belonging to the Commonwealth situated at the junction of Main and Fort Point channels, bounded south-westerly by the flats of the Boston Wharf Company, and south-easterly by the said flats sold to said Boston and Albany Railroad Company, a strip along the south-easterly margin of said flats of the Commonwealth, bounded south-easterly by said flats sold to said Railroad Company under said agreement of said 8th of December, and included by parallel lines extending from said flats of said Boston Wharf Company to the exterior line defined in said agreement, so drawn as to include an area amounting to two-fifths of the area herein surrendered by said Boston and Albany Railroad Company, from its purchase under said agreement.

And said Commonwealth and said Boston and Albany Railroad Company hereby mutually agree, each with the other, that the provisions of said agreement of said 8th of December, as modified by these presents, shall apply to said strip of flats to be conveyed to said Company in place of, and as an equivalent for, the said flats, herein surrendered to said Commonwealth, to the same extent in all respects, except as herein provided, as though such strip were included within the original tract of flats to which said agreement relates ; and they further agree to define specifically, by metes and bounds, said strip, as soon as Eastern Avenue shall be located under said indenture of four parts.

And said Commonwealth hereby further agrees with said Company, that it will convey to said Company in fee, at the rate of twenty cents for every square foot, such an area of the territory described in said agreement of said 8th of December, lying south-west of Eastern Avenue, as located under said indenture of four parts, and north-west of the extension of B Street, not exceeding forty feet in width, as said Company shall take for a road-bed for its tracks ; and said Company hereby agrees with said Commonwealth, that it will fill such area, so taken for a road-bed, in accordance with the obligations of said Company for filling the area to be conveyed to it lying north-east of Eastern Avenue, and that it will locate its said road-bed for tracks south-west of Eastern Avenue, over the territory of the Commonwealth, on or before the said first day of October, 1876 :

Provided, however, that should Eastern Avenue be located over the territory described in said agreement of said 8th of December farther north than it is located according to the plan for the occupation of flats owned by the Commonwealth in Boston Harbor appended to the Sixth Annual Report of the Board of Harbor Commissioners, said Company shall, if required by said Board, take the additional area of such territory brought south of Eastern Avenue by the change from the location shown on said plan, in a strip of the same area, of equal width, along the south-easterly line of its territory, as limited by such new location ; or, at the option of said Boston and Albany Railroad Company, said Company shall be entitled to have deducted from the purchase-money said Company is to pay said Commonwealth the value of such additional area that shall be brought south of Eastern Avenue by such change of location, and in consequence surrendered, from the amount purchased by said Company, reckoning such value at twenty cents per square foot.

And said Commonwealth hereby further agrees with said Boston and Albany Railroad Company, that in case said Company shall reserve a portion of its said flats at the south-easterly corner of the same for a dock, and build the wall for such dock on the north-westerly and south-westerly sides of such portion so reserved, then said Company shall be exempt from the obligation to fill on the south-easterly boundary line of such area, for the protection of filling in the adjoining territory, as provided in said agreement of said 8th of December.

And said Commonwealth hereby further agrees with said Company, that in making the determination of the amount to be added to, or deducted from, the purchase-money, after the survey provided in said agreement of the 8th of December, there shall be deducted from the amount of such purchase-money the cost of the wall built by said Company along the north-easterly border of said westerly strip to be conveyed as herein provided to said Company, determining said cost at the average rate of the contract price said Company shall pay for the wall to be built by it along the north-easterly margin of its whole tract purchased under said agreement and these presents ; and that there shall further be deducted from such purchase-money one-half the cost of the filling of Eastern Avenue on the territory of said Company, estimating such cost at the average contract price said Company shall pay for the filling of its said territory purchased of said Commonwealth.

And said Commonwealth hereby further agrees with said Boston and Albany Railroad Company, that in case Northern Avenue, Eastern Avenue, or the extension of B Street within the limits of the territory to be conveyed to said Company, shall be laid out, under said indenture of four parts, to a greater width than is stipulated in said agreement of said 8th of December, said Company shall not be liable to pay, under said agreement, for the additional area appropriated to such streets by such increase of their width.

And said Commonwealth hereby further agrees, for the purpose of avoiding the necessity of building bulkheads on the north-westerly division line of the territory of said Company, to retain the filling when done by said Company on such line; that it and its assigns will fill upon said north-westerly division line between the territory to be conveyed to said Company and the territory of the Commonwealth adjacent, simultaneously with the progress of filling on said line by said Company, upon twenty days' notice in writing of the intention of said Company so to fill on such line; provided that said Commonwealth nor said Company shall be required so to fill, until the sea-wall on the north-westerly and north-easterly borders of the territory of the Commonwealth is so far built as to furnish a protection to the filling on such division line from the currents of the channels of Boston Harbor.

And said Commonwealth and said Boston and Albany Railroad Company bind themselves, each to the other, to the faithful performance of their respective agreements hereinbefore set forth, and of their respective obligations under said agreement dated December 8, A.D. 1869, as herein modified, firmly by these presents.

In testimony whereof, the said Commonwealth has caused its corporate seal to be hereto affixed, and these presents to be signed, acknowledged, and delivered, in its name and behalf, by Josiah Quincy, Frederic W. Lincoln, Joshua N. Marshall, and William T. Grammer, its Harbor Commissioners, the same to be approved by its Governor and Executive Council, and the said Boston and Albany Railroad Company has caused its corporate seal to be hereto affixed, and these presents to be signed, acknowledged, and delivered, in its name and behalf, by Chester W. Chapin, its president, thereunto duly authorized by the vote of the directors of said Company, a copy of which is hereto annexed, this twenty-fourth day of June, A.D. eighteen hundred and seventy-three.

COMMONWEALTH OF MASSACHUSETTS, [SEAL.]

By JOSIAH QUINCY.

F. W. LINCOLN.

W. T. GRAMMER.

J. N. MARSHALL.

Signed, sealed, and delivered in presence of
HENRY L. WHITING.

BOSTON AND ALBANY RAILROAD COMPANY, [SEAL.]

By C. W. CHAPIN, *President.*

In presence of ERASTUS HAYES.

COMMONWEALTH OF MASSACHUSETTS.

IN COUNCIL, July 15, 1873.

OLIVER WARNER, *Secretary.*

Approved:

4

AGREEMENT BETWEEN THE COMMONWEALTH AND MESSRS. CLAPP & BALLOU AND THE ROCKPORT GRANITE COMPANY OF MASSACHUSETTS.

ARTICLES OF AGREEMENT,

Made this twenty-ninth day of September, in the year eighteen hundred and seventy-three, by and between the Rockport Granite Company of Massachusetts, a corporation established under the laws of the Commonwealth of Massachusetts, George Clapp, and Frederick R. Ballou, both of Boston, in the county of Suffolk and said Commonwealth, partners under the firm and style of Clapp & Ballou, the said Rockport Granite Company and Clapp & Ballou being parties of the first part, and the Commonwealth of Massachusetts, acting by its Board of Harbor Commissioners, party of the second part, *Witness:*

The said parties of the first part hereby covenant and agree with said party of the second part to build two sea-walls, one a light sea-wall, the other a heavy sea-wall, on a parcel of land and flats belonging to the party of the second part, situated in Boston Harbor, and bounded south-westerly by land and flats of the Boston Wharf Company, north-westerly by Fort Point Channel, north-easterly by the main channel, and south-easterly by land and flats sold by said party of the second part to the Boston and Albany Railroad Company, the north-westerly boundary line of which is to be hereafter defined, and to fill said parcel with solid material to the grade of sixteen feet above mean low water, in the manner and upon the terms and conditions following:

First. The base of said light sea-wall shall commence at a point marked X, on annexed plan marked C, twenty-five feet easterly of the Commissioners' line, on the easterly side of Fort Point Channel, established by chapter 35 of the Acts of the year 1840, and thence extending, as shown by the red line on annexed plan marked C, parallel to said Commissioners' line of 1840, and the modified line of 1867, to a point three hundred and eighty-seven and a half feet northerly from Commissioners' line B, said point to be subject to alteration by the engineer of the Board of Harbor Commissioners.

Said wall shall be built in accordance with the plan marked D, hereto annexed, and in such location as shall be marked out by the engineer of the Board of Harbor Commissioners previous to the commencement of operations by the parties of the first part; and the parties of the first part shall preserve the location of said line by driving piles to mark the location of the wall permanently.

The trench shall be dredged for the wall, under the direction of said engineer, to a depth of two feet below low water, spring tides.

The foundation piles to support the wall shall occupy a space nine feet wide, having five piles in parallel rows, said rows to be two and one-half feet distant from centre to centre of each row.

All piles shall be driven into the hard clay stratum to the satisfaction of the engineer of the Harbor Commissioners; the piles to be in diameter not less than ten inches at low-water mark, spring tides, at which point they are to be sawed off level with each other.

On the top of the piles are to be spiked two layers of spruce plank, twelve inches wide and three inches thick, lying at right angles with each other; the space between the heads of the piles, for two feet in depth, to be filled and well rammed with stone-chip ballast or oyster-shells.

The wall, from low water of spring-tides to the top of the coping-stones, or grade sixteen, shall be eighteen feet in height, with a true batter front and rear. The wall shall be nine feet wide at the bottom, and five feet wide at the top, including an offset of one foot for a resting-place for cap to support the ends of platform-joists; to be constructed of good quality granite rubble-wall stones, from eighteen inches to two feet thick, with sufficient headers to secure the stability of the wall, well bonded and pinned throughout.

The rear of the wall shall be ballasted with oyster-shells from the back of the wall to a line commencing at a point two feet in rear of the back of the top of the wall, and extending in a slope of forty-five degrees to the base of the wall, as shown on said annexed plan marked D.

At the end of the wall a flank wall shall be built, to connect this wall with the adjoining heavy sea-wall, according to the direction of the engineer of the Board of Harbor Commissioners.

This wall to be commenced within thirty days after notice that the location of the wall is made, and the work to be prosecuted without delay to its completion, and completed on or before the first day of May, eighteen hundred and seventy-four.

Second. The base of the heavy sea-wall shall be built on a line parallel to said modified line of 1867, and one foot within the same, as aforesaid, as shown by red line on said plan C, and in such location as shall be marked out by the engineer of the Board of Harbor Commissioners previous to the commencement of operations by the parties of the first part; and the parties of the first part shall preserve the location of said line by driving piles to mark the location of the wall permanently. This sea-wall shall be built in accordance with the plan marked G, hereto annexed. The trench for this sea-wall shall be excavated, to the satisfaction of said engineer, forty-five feet in width at the bottom, which shall be as nearly as practicable a level surface. The depth of the trench shall be at least twenty-three feet below mean low water, and always to hard bottom.

This trench is to be filled with broken quarry-stones of mixed sizes, none less than seventy-five pounds' weight, thrown in and deposited in regular layers of not over four feet each in depth, and each layer is to be placed compactly by divers with bars before depositing the next layer.

This filling is to be forty-five feet in width at the bottom and for the lower three feet of its depth, thence sloping inward on each side with a slope of one and a half horizontal to one vertical for a further depth of nine feet, where, at a level of eleven feet below mean low water, it is to be eighteen feet in width. The filling is to be levelled up here with smaller chips of quarry-stone to receive the wall, and the outer or harbor slope is to have the interstices well filled with similar chips.

The wall to the height of one foot below low water shall be built in quarry-face dimension-stone of granite, laid in courses of two feet rise each, by the aid of submarine divers. The courses shall be laid alternately, entirely with headers and stretchers, the bottom or first course being headers. Each stone shall be at least four feet and not more than ten feet long, at least eighteen inches wide, and exactly two feet rise, fitted to one-inch joints, square ends, and out of wind.

The wall shall be compactly laid in a substantial and workman-like manner, with fair and close outer face. Stones shall be laid so as to break joints everywhere, with good and sufficient bearing upon the beds without pinners.

The base of the wall shall be fourteen feet; the height of the wall, to one foot below mean low water, ten feet; and the thickness of the wall, at top, eleven feet four inches.

The wall, from one foot below mean low water to the top of the coping-stones, or grade sixteen, shall be laid with dimension-stone in cement. The courses shall be laid with headers and stretchers, with not over ten feet interval between the headers, and have two feet rise, with the exception of the coping-course, which shall have a rise of three feet, and be entirely of headers. The stretchers shall be at least four feet long, and the headers shall not be less than six feet long from face inwardly. The batter of each face shall be two inches to the foot. The base of this wall shall be nine feet eight inches, the height seventeen feet, and the thickness at the top of the wall five feet.

The back of the whole of the heavy wall, from top to bottom, shall be ballasted with clean gravel, cobbles, or oyster-shells, resting at a slope as steep as they will stand, or forty-five degrees, and tapering to nothing at the top of the wall.

This heavy sea-wall shall be commenced by the first day of May, 1874, and finished by the first day of August, 1875.

Third. Spaces in said walls for docks, or for the purpose of filling by scows, or any other purpose, may at any time be reserved permanently or temporarily by said Board of Harbor Commissioners, upon notice before the structure of the wall is begun in any such space; and, where such space is permanently reserved, it shall be filled by a strong bulkhead, to the satisfaction of the said engineer.

Fourth. The filling on said parcel of land and flats must be up to grade sixteen. Up to grade thirteen the filling must be with materials dredged from the mouth of Fort Point Channel, below the line of Oliver Street extended, and from that part of Boston Harbor represented by the space colored red on the " Plan for the occupation of flats owned by the Commonwealth in Boston Harbor," appended to the Sixth Annual Report of the Board of Harbor Commissioners, and other portions of Boston Harbor above a line extended from Buoy No. 11 at right angles with the line of said heavy sea-wall on the main channel. All such portions of Boston Harbor are to be dredged to a uniform depth of twenty-three feet at mean low water. Such portion of Fort Point Channel is to be so dredged that the bottom shall uniformly and gradually slope from a depth of twelve feet at mean low water at the line of Oliver Street to a depth of twenty-three feet at the south-west border of the area represented by the space colored red on said plan. The residue of the filling to grade sixteen must be with good clean gravel.

All material obtained from the dredging required by this agreement may be used as filling, except above grade thirteen. The whole filling to be finished on or before October 1, 1876. Where the said sea-walls to be built around said flats shall not be built so as to furnish the requisite protection to the filling, temporary bulkheads must be built for that purpose, as required by the Board of Harbor Commissioners. Spaces required for docks may be reserved at any time from filling by the Board of Harbor Commissioners.

Fifth. Both the dredging and the filling shall be done according to the direction of the Board of Harbor Commissioners.

And said parties of the first part further covenant and agree with said party of the second part to give the Board of Harbor Commissioners and its agents every facility that may be required by said Board for the inspection of materials to be used and of the work done by said parties under this agreement and while such work is in progress ; and also agree, if, at any time during the progress of the work, any work shall be done or any material used which shall be considered by the engineer of said Board unfit and inferior according to the true intent of this agreement, that, upon receiving notice thereof, they will forthwith remove such objectionable work or material, and substitute other in its place which shall be satisfactory to such engineer.

The said party of the second part hereby covenants and agrees with said parties of the first part to pay said parties for building said sea-walls and filling said land and flats in the manner and upon the terms and conditions herein set forth and agreed as follows : —

For the light sea-wall, at the rate of thirty-nine dollars for every lineal foot of finished wall.

For the heavy sea-wall, at the rate of two hundred and thirty-six dollars for every lineal foot of finished wall.

For the filling up of said parcel of land and flats with dredged material and good clean gravel, as herein agreed, at the rate of thirty-nine cents for every superficial foot of said territory so filled according to the measurement of the same by the engineer of the Board of Harbor Commissioners, on the completion of the whole contract. In determining the whole amount to be paid for the fill-

ing by measuring on the surface inside the top of the sea-walls, a
deduction shall be made at the rate of fifty-nine cents per cubic
yard for the number of cubic yards of ballast, foundation, and
other material constituting the walls, that would otherwise, by a
superficial measurement of the filling, be reckoned as a part of
such filling.

Payments will be made every month for the work performed under
this contract to the satisfaction of the engineer of the Board, at
the rate of ninety per cent of the contract price of the work done
during the month as reported and certified to by the said engineer,
and upon the approval of the bills by the Board of Harbor Commissioners and the Governor and Council. Such payments may be
made to and receipted for by some party authorized to receipt for
the same by an instrument in writing duly executed by said parties of the first part.

And said party of the second part further agrees, that said parties of the first part, in performing the work herein contracted for,
may have the benefit of and exercise the rights secured to said
party of the second part and its assigns by certain provisions of
an indenture of four parts, dated the twenty-fourth day of June,
A.D. 1873, made by and between said party of the second part,
the Boston and Albany Railroad Company, the Boston Wharf
Company, and the City of Boston, whereby said Boston Wharf
Company made certain covenants and agreements with said party
of the second part in relation to filling on the division line between said land and flats of the Boston Wharf Company and the
lands and flats of said party of the second part, and in relation to
the building of bulkheads or barriers on said line to retain the filling, and in relation to a right of way secured to said party of the
second part and its assigns, from the track of the New York and
New England Railroad to the territory to be filled under this
agreement, and in relation to the right to lay railroad tracks over
the territory of said Boston Wharf Company for the transportation in cars of material to be used in filling said territory of said
party of the second part. It is, however, understood and agreed
by and between the parties hereto, that, whatever the parties of
the first part may do in the exercise of said rights secured as aforesaid to the party of the second part and its assigns, the said parties of the first part shall do at their own proper cost and expense,
and that said party of the second part shall be in no respect responsible for them or their action, or any liabilities whatever which
they may incur.

It is further agreed by and between the parties hereto, that whenever the appropriations of the Legislature now or hereafter made for the work herein contracted for shall become exhausted before the work is completed, then no more work shall be done, and neither of said parties shall be under any obligation to pro-, ceed further under this agreement; but, so long as there shall be appropriations of the Legislature from which the work as it is done can be paid for from month to month as herein provided, this agreement shall be in full force and virtue.

It is further agreed by and between said parties hereto, that any person shall be deemed the engineer of the Board of Harbor Commissioners, within the meaning of this agreement, whom said Board shall at any time, or from time to time, designate for the performance of any service it may desire in relation to the work to be done under this agreement.

It is further agreed by and between said parties hereto, that the Harbor Commissioners, subject to the approval of the Governor and Council, shall have the right to make changes in the plan of doing said work, should occasion arise, and make such additions to and reductions from the contract price as shall be just to both parties.

It is further agreed by and between said parties hereto, that should the parties of the first part refuse or neglect to execute according to this agreement the work herein contracted for, or fail to prosecute with the requisite vigor to insure its completion within the time agreed upon, or in any other respect violate this agreement, the Board of Harbor Commissioners shall have the power to annul this agreement, and to contract anew with other parties.

It is further agreed by and between said parties hereto, that in case any difference shall arise under this agreement between the parties of the first part and the party of the second part, acting by the Board of Harbor Commissioners, that the said parties of the first part and said Board are unable to settle and adjust, the same shall be finally determined upon hearing by the Governor and Council.

In testimony whereof, the Rockport Granite Company aforesaid has caused its corporate seal to be hereto affixed, and these presents to be signed and delivered in its name and behalf, by John Stimson, its treasurer, and the said George Clapp and Frederick K. Ballou have hereunto set their hands and seals, and the said Commonwealth has caused its corporate seal to be hereto affixed, and these presents to be signed and delivered in its name and behalf, by Joshua Quincy, Darwin E. Ware, Frederic W. Lincoln, Joshua N. Marshall, and William T. Grammer, its Harbor Commissioners, and the same to be approved by its Governor and Executive Council, the day and year first above written.

Signed, sealed, and delivered in the presence of
E. C. PERKINS.

ROCKPORT GRANITE COMPANY OF MASSACHUSETTS,

By JOHN STIMSON, *Treasurer.* [Seal.]

GEORGE CLAPP. [Seal.]

F. K. BALLOU. [Seal.]

COMMONWEALTH OF MASSACHUSETTS, [Seal.]

HENRY MITCHELL.

, By JOSHUA QUINCY.

DARWIN E. WARE.

F. W. LINCOLN.

J. N. MARSHALL.

W. T. GRAMMER.

IN COUNCIL, October 10, 1873.

Approved: OLIVER WARNER, *Secretary of the Commonwealth.*

BOND.

Know all men by these Presents, That we, the Rockport Granite Company of Massachusetts, a corporation established under the laws of the Commonwealth of Massachusetts, George Clapp and Frederick K. Ballou, both of Boston, in the county of Suffolk and said Commonwealth, partners under the firm and style of Clapp & Ballou, as principals, and Aaron W. Russell and Jesse Buntin, both of Quincy, in the county of Norfolk and said Commonwealth, Asa C. Sanborn of Cambridge, in the county of Middlesex in said Commonwealth, John Stimson and John H. Stimson, both of said Boston, as sureties, are holden and stand firmly bound unto the Commonwealth of Massachusetts in the sum of two hundred and fifty thousand dollars, to the payment of which to the said Commonwealth of Massachusetts we hereby jointly and severally bind ourselves, our successors, heirs, executors, and administrators.

The condition of this obligation is such, that if the above-

5

bounden Rockport Granite Company, Clapp and Ballou, shall faithfully, well, and truly perform their obligations under the foregoing
agreement, made by and between them and the said Commonwealth, of even date with these presents, and shall do or cause to
be done according to the requirements of said agreement, in the
manner and upon the terms and conditions therein set forth, all
the work in said agreement contracted for, then this obligation
shall be void; otherwise remain in full force and virtue.

In witness whereof, the said Rockport Granite Company has
caused its corporate seal to be hereto affixed, and these presents to
be signed and delivered, by John Stimson, its Treasurer, thereunto
duly authorized, and we, the said George Clapp and Frederick
K. Ballou, Aaron W. Russell, Jesse Buntin, Asa C. Sanborn,
John Stimson, and John H. Stimson, have hereunto set our hands
and seals, this twenty-ninth day of September, A.D. eighteen
hundred and seventy-three.

Signed, sealed, and delivered in the presence of
E. C. Perkins.

ROCKPORT GRANITE COMPANY OF MASSACHUSETTS,

John Stimson, *Treasurer.*	[Seal.]
George Clapp.	[Seal.]
F. K. Ballou.	[Seal.]
A. C. Sanborn.	[Seal.]
John Stimson.	[Seal.]
Jesse Buntin.	[Seal.]
John H. Stimson.	[Seal.]
A. W. Russell.	[Seal.]

In Council, Oct. 10, 1873.

Approved: OLIVER WARNER, *Secretary of the Commonwealth.*

ARTICLES OF AGREEMENT,

Made this thirteenth day of June, A.D. 1875, by and between George Clapp and Frederick K. Ballou, both of Boston and the county of Suffolk and said Commonwealth, partners under the firm and style of Clapp & Ballou, being parties of the first part, and the Commonwealth of Massachusetts, acting by its Board of Harbor Commissioners, party of the second part,

WITNESS:

The said parties of the first part hereby covenant and agree with the said party of the second part to build a light sea-wall, to enclose a dock, upon a parcel of land and flats belonging to the party of the second part, situated in Boston Harbor, as follows : —

Beginning at a point in the line of the heavy sea-wall now being constructed, distant two hundred and twenty-two and one-half feet (222½) westerly from the boundary line of flats sold to the Boston and Albany Railroad Corporation. The central axis of said dock shall lie parallel with said boundary line. The side walls of the dock shall be connected to the heavy sea-wall on each side, at which point the dock shall have an opening of one hundred and forty-five feet between the timber platforms and an opening of two hundred and twenty-five feet between its side walls and their top line, the said timber platforms being intended to be forty feet wide at this point, on each side. The length of the dock shall be eight hundred and fifty feet from the face of the heavy sea-wall back to the cross-wall at the head of the dock, measuring on the axis of the dock at the level of the top of the walls. The side walls shall be built upon such curved lines as may be given by the engineers hereinafter named, and shall be symmetrically placed on each side the axis of the dock. The width of the dock at its inner ·end shall be one hundred and twenty-five feet (125) between the timber platforms, and one hundred and sixty-five (165') between its walls, the said platforms being intended here to be twenty feet wide on each side. The cross-walls shall be at right angles with the axis, and bonded into the side walls.

Said walls shall be built in accordance with the plan of light sea-wall bound into the eighth annual report of the Board of Harbor Commissioners, except that the ballast behind the same may be of gravel, placed at such slope as it will assume, and extending to the top. It shall be built in such location as shall be marked out by the engineer of the Board of Harbor Commissioners previous to the commencement of operations by the parties of the first part; and the parties of the first part shall preserve the location by driving piles to hold the lines permanently.

The trench shall be dredged for the wall, under the direction of said engineer, to a depth of two feet below low water, spring tides. The foundation piles to support the wall shall occupy a space ten feet wide, having five piles in parallel rows, said rows to be two and one-half feet distant from centre to centre of each row.

All piles shall be driven into the hard clay stratum to the satisfaction of the engineer of the Harbor Commissioners. The piles to be in diameter not less than ten inches at low-water mark, spring tides; at which point they are to be sawed off level with each other.

On the top of the piles are to be spiked two layers of spruce plank, twelve inches wide and three inches thick, lying at right angles with each other. The space between the heads of the piles, for two feet in depth, to be filled and well rammed with stone-chip ballast or oyster-shells.

The wall, from low water of spring tides to the top of the coping-stones or grade sixteen, shall be eighteen feet in height, with a true batter front and rear. The wall shall be nine feet wide at the bottom, and five feet wide at the top, including an offset of one foot for a resting-place for cap to support the ends of platform joists; to be constructed of good quality granite rubble-wall stones from one foot to three feet thick, with sufficient headers to secure stability of the wall, well bonded and pinned throughout.

The rear of the wall shall be ballasted with oyster-shells, broken stone or gravel, from the back of the wall to a line commencing at a point two feet in rear of the back of the top of the wall, and extending in a natural slope to the base of the wall.

At the end of the wall a flank shall be built, to connect this wall with the adjoining heavy sea-wall, according to the direction of the engineer of the Board of Harbor Commissioners.

Near the junction of the dock walls and the heavy sea-wall, riprap of broken stone of mixed sizes shall be applied in such place and in such manner as directed by the engineer in charge of the work, on the outer face of the foundation, under the intended platform.

This wall to be commenced at once, and the work to be prosecuted without delay to its completion, and completed on or before the first day of July, in the year eighteen hundred and seventy-six.

All material obtained from the dredging required by this agreement may be used as filling, except above grade thirteen.

And said parties of the first part further covenant and agree with said party of the second part to give the Board of Harbor Commis-

sioners and its agents every facility that may be required by said
Board for the inspection of materials to be used and of the work
done by said parties under this agreement and while such work is
in progress; and also agree, if, at any time during the progress of
the work, any work shall be done or any material used which shall
be considered by the engineer of said Board unfit and inferior
according to the true intent of this agreement, that, upon receiving
notice thereof, they will forthwith remove such objectionable work
or material, and substitute other in its place which shall be satisfactory to such engineer.

The said party of the second part hereby covenants and agrees
with said parties of the first part to pay said parties for building
said sea-walls in the manner and upon the terms and conditions
herein set forth and agreed, as follows: At the rate of thirty-nine
dollars for every lineal foot of finished wall, and at the rate of one
dollar and twenty-five cents per ton of certified weight of rip-rap
in front of foundation.

Payments will be made every month for the work performed
under this contract to the satisfaction of the engineer of the Board,
at the rate of ninety per cent of the contract price of the work
done during the month as reported and certified to by the said
engineer, and upon the approval of the bills by the Board of Harbor Commissioners and the Governor and Council. Such payments
may be made to and receipted for by some party authorized to
receipt for the same by an instrument in writing duly executed by
said parties of the first part.

It is further agreed by and between the parties hereto, that
whenever the appropriations of the Legislature now or hereafter
made for the work herein contracted for shall become exhausted
before the work is completed, then no more work shall be done,
and neither of said parties shall be under any obligation to proceed
further under this agreement; but so long as there shall be appropriations of the Legislature from which the work as it is done can
be paid for from month to month as herein provided, this agreement shall be in full force and virtue.

It is further agreed by and between said parties hereto, that
any person shall be deemed the engineer of the Board of Harbor
Commissioners, within the meaning of this agreement, whom said
Board shall at any time, or from time to time, designate for the
performance of any service it may desire in relation to the work to
be done under this agreement.

It is further agreed by and between said parties hereto, that the
Harbor Commissioners, subject to the approval of the Governor
and Council, shall have the right to make changes in the plan of
doing said work, should occasion arise, and make such additions

to and reductions from the contract price as shall be just to both parties.

It is further agreed by and between said parties hereto, that should the parties of the first part refuse or neglect to execute, according to this agreement, the work herein contracted for, or fail to prosecute with the requisite vigor to insure its completion within the time agreed upon, or in any other respect violate this agreement, the Board of Harbor Commissioners shall have the power to annul this agreement, and to contract anew with other parties.

It is further agreed by and between said parties hereto, that in case any difference shall arise under this agreement between the parties of the first part and the party of the second part, acting by the Board of Harbor Commissioners, that the said parties of the first part and said Board are unable to settle and adjust, the same shall be finally determined upon hearing by the Governor and Council.

In testimony whereof, the said George Clapp and Frederick K. Ballou have hereunto set their hands and seals, and the said Commonwealth has caused its corporate seal to be hereto affixed, and these presents to be signed and delivered in its name and behalf, by Josiah Quincy, Albert Mason, Frederic W. Lincoln, Joshua N. Marshall, and William T. Grammer, its Harbor Commissioners, and the same to be approved by its Governor and Executive Council, the day and year first above written.

GEORGE CLAPP.   [SEAL.]

FREDERICK K. BALLOU.   [SEAL.]

COMMONWEALTH OF MASSACHUSETTS,

By JOSIAH QUINCY.

FREDERIC W. LINCOLN.

JOSHUA N. MARSHALL.

WILLIAM T. GRAMMER.

ALBERT MASON.

Signed, sealed, and delivered in the presence of [the word "*thirtieth*" first written over an erasure, the words "*eleven*" and "*ten*" and nine other words first scored, and the words "*hereinafter named*," "*ten*," and "*nine*," first interlined, also the words "*eighteen inches to two*" first scored, and "*one foot to three*" first interlined]

HENRY L. WHITING.   [SEAL.]

Approved in Council, June 30, 1875.

OLIVER WARNER, *Secretary*.

BOND.

KNOW ALL MEN BY THESE PRESENTS:

That George Clapp and Frederick K. Ballou, both of Boston, in the county of Suffolk and Commonwealth of Massachusetts, partners under the firm and style of Clapp & Ballou, as principals, and George W. Townsend of said Boston, and Joshua Phillips of Weymouth, in the county of Norfolk, as sureties, are holden and stand firmly bound and obliged unto the Commonwealth of Massachusetts in the full and just sum of twenty-five thousand dollars, to be paid unto the said Commonwealth of Massachusetts; to which payment well and truly to be made we bind ourselves, heirs, executors, and administrators, firmly by these presents.

Sealed with our seals. Dated the thirtieth day of June, in the year of our Lord one thousand eight hundred and seventy-five.

The condition of this obligation is such, that if the above-bounden Clapp & Ballou shall faithfully, well, and truly perform their obligations under the agreement of even date with these presents, made by and between them and the said Commonwealth, for the construction of a dock in connection with work in progress upon the Commonwealth flats at South Boston, and shall do or cause to be done according to the requirements of said agreement, in the manner and upon the terms and conditions therein set forth, all the work in said agreement contracted for, then this obligation shall be void; otherwise remain in full force and virtue.

> GEORGE CLAPP.   [SEAL.]
> FREDERICK K. BALLOU.   [SEAL.]
> GEO. W. TOWNSEND.   [SEAL.]
> JOSHUA PHILLIPS.   [SEAL.]

Signed, sealed, and delivered, four printed words first erased, in presence of   A. D. McCLELLAN.

Approved in Council, June 30, 1875.

OLIVER WARNER, *Secretary*.

[Copy.]

BOSTON AND ALBANY RAILROAD COMPANY, {
OFFICE OF SECRETARY, SPRINGFIELD, MASS., Nov. 2, 1877. }

I hereby certify that at a meeting of the Board of Directors of the Boston and Albany Railroad Company duly held in the city of Boston, on the twenty-fifth day of October, 1877, the following vote was passed : —

" Whereas, The agreement between the Commonwealth of Massachusetts and the Boston and Albany Railroad Company, dated on the twenty-fourth day of June, A.D. 1873, printed in the Appendix to the Eighth Annual Report of the Board of Harbor Commissioners of said Commonwealth, does, by the clause thereof beginning " Provided, however," contained in the last seventeen lines of the fifty-eighth page of said Report, provide that said company shall either take a certain additional area of territory, in a strip of land described in said clause, or at the option of said company have deducted from the purchase-money mentioned in said clause the value, at the rate of twenty cents per square foot, of the additional area of territory last mentioned in said clause: Now, then,

"*Voted*, on motion of Mr. Kimball, That said company will and does hereby elect to have said value so deducted at said rate from said purchase-money, and not to take said strip ; and that notice of this such election be given to said Commonwealth and said Commissioners by sending to said Commissioners a copy of this vote."

A true copy.

Attest :   J. A. RUMRILL,
Clerk B. & A. R.R. Co.

BOSTON, Nov. 1st, 1877.

To the Honorable Board of Land Commissioners.

The undersigned, in behalf of the Boston and Albany Railroad Company, respectfully represent, —

That by an agreement made on the eighth day of December, A.D. 1869, by and between the Commonwealth of Massachusetts, acting by its Board of Harbor Commissioners, and the Boston and Albany Railroad Company, the said Commonwealth agreed, that in six years from the first day of October, 1869, it would convey to said Railroad Company a certain parcel of flats in South Boston therein particularly

Fourth Report HarborCommis-sioners, page 99.

described, said conveyance to be made upon certain conditions therein contained; and the said Boston and Albany Railroad Company therein agreed that it would pay to said *Fourth Report* Commonwealth in three years from said first day of *Harbor Commissioners, page* October, for said parcel of flats, the sum of $435,600. *101.* in cash or the bonds of said Company; and it was further agreed that said flats so to be conveyed and paid for should, when filled, be surveyed by the engineer of said Board of Harbor Commissioners, and that said sum of $435,600 should be increased or diminished at the rate of twenty cents a square foot, accord- *Fourth Report,* ing as the number of feet, exclusive of Northern and *page 104.* Eastern Avenues, and the extension of B Street, should be found more or less than fifty acres.

That by a supplementary agreement made between said Commonwealth and said Boston and Albany Railroad *Eighth Report,* Company, dated June 24, 1873, said original contract *page 56.* was modified and changed, whereby it was provided that a portion of said flats lying south-west of the south-westerly *Eighth Report,* line of Eastern Avenue should be exchanged for a *page 57.* strip of flats situated at the junction of Main and Fort Point Channels, bounded south-easterly by the flats previously sold to said Railroad Company, in the proportion of five (5) feet of said flats surrendered by said Railroad Company for two (2) feet of said flats to be taken in exchange therefor.

And it was further stipulated in said supplementary agreement, that should Eastern Avenue be located over the terri- *Eighth Report,* tory described in said agreement of December, 1869, *page 58.* farther north than it was located according to the plan appended to the Sixth Annual Report of said Harbor Commissioners, said Boston and Albany Railroad Company shall be entitled, at its option, to have deducted from the purchase-money said Company is to pay said Commonwealth the value of such area as shall be brought south of Eastern Avenue.

And it was further provided, that there should be deducted from the amount of said purchase-money the cost of the *Eighth Report,* heavy sea-wall to be built by said Company along the *page 59.* north-easterly line of said westerly strip of flats to be conveyed to said Company in exchange for the area south of Eastern Avenue, estimating said cost at the average rate of the contract price paid by said Company for said wall.

And it was also provided that there shall be deducted from said purchase-money one-half of the cost of filling said *Eighth Report,* Eastern Avenue, which filling said Company is to do. *page 59.*

Now, therefore, the undersigned, in behalf of said Boston and Albany Railroad Company, respectfully represent that said Railroad Company has elected to have deducted from the purchase-money said Company was to pay to said Commonwealth the value of the area brought south of Eastern Avenue by the change of the location of said avenue, which said area contains 128,000 square feet, amounting, at twenty cents a foot, to the sum of $25,600.

That, as nearly as can now be determined by the measurement and estimates made by the engineer of said Board of Harbor Commissioners, the whole area to be conveyed to said Company by said Commonwealth, under and by virtue of the aforesaid agreements, after deducting said 128,000 feet, is 1,793,524 square feet, of which area 126,984 feet are to be paid for at fifty cents a foot, amounting to $63,492, and 1,668,540 feet at twenty cents a foot, amounting to $333,708, making the total price $397,200.

That said area, as measured by said engineer, includes the area embraced within the limits of Northern Avenue, and of the extension of B Street, which by the terms of said original agreement are expressly excluded from the area of flats to be paid for by said Company (see Fourth Report of Harbor Commissioners, page 12, at bottom, and 104, fourteenth line).

The area included within Northern Avenue is 95,000 feet, and in the extension of B Street is 45,000 feet; total, in both, 140,000 feet.

That said Railroad Company is further entitled to be credited with the cost of building a heavy sea-wall along the north-easterly margin of said westerly strip as provided in said agreement of June, 1873, at the average cost of said wall; viz., 96½ feet at $236, or $22,974.

And that said Company is further entitled to an allowance for one-half of the cost of filling Eastern Avenue (see Eighth Report, page 59).

The area of Eastern Avenue against said Company's flats is 880 feet by 75 feet, or 66,000 square feet. The cost of filling one-half of this area, or 33,000 feet, at thirty-nine cents a superficial foot, which is the contract price, will be $12,870.

The undersigned also represent that by said supplementary agreement of June 24, 1873, the term of payment of the purchase-money, stipulated in said agreement of December 8, 1869, and the time for doing such work, as was required in said agreement, was extended to the first day of October, 1876; and all claim for interest on said purchase-money which accrued before said last mentioned date was released.

The statement of the account of said Boston and Albany Railroad Company with the Commonwealth for said flats will be substantially as follows : —

B. & A. R.R. Co. TO COMMONWEALTH, DR.

To whole area, exclusive of territory south of Eastern Avenue, by measurement of engineer, . 1,793,524 feet.

1,668,540 ft. @ 20 cts., ...	$333,708	
126,984 ft. @ 50 cts., ...	63,492	
		$397,200
Credits and allowances: —		
Area included in Northern Avenue, —		
86,400 ft. @ 20 cts., ...	$17,280	
9,600 ft. @ 50 cts., ...	4,800	
Extension of B Street, —		
45,000 ft. @ 20 cts., ...	9,000	
Cost of heavy sea-wall, —		
96½ ft. @ $236, ...	22,774	
One-half cost of filling Eastern Avenue, —		
33,000 ft. @ 39 cts., ...	12,870	
		66,724
Balance due, ...		$330,476

The whole area of flats to be conveyed to the Railroad Company has not been filled ; nor has the sea-wall been built in strict conformity with the provisions of the agreement with the Commonwealth, dated June 24, 1873 ; neither has the Commonwealth, doubtless for good and sufficient reasons, complied strictly with its own obligations as to the work to be performed on its part ; and, if the work incumbent on the Railroad Company had been fully performed, their flats would have been entirely useless, on account of the non-performance by the Commonwealth of its portion of the work. The Railroad Company entered upon the work of improvement in good faith in 1873, and has expended upon the flats to the present time about $92,458, exclusive of interest.

When the contract of June, 1873, was made, the business of the Railroad Company was at its maximum, the gross income of the road in that year being $9,798,000, and the gross tons of freight moved 2,884,000. Since that time there has been a large shrinkage in business and income each year, until 1876, when the gross income of the road fell to $7,074,000, and the tons of freight moved to 2,541,000.

Under these altered circumstances, to have pressed forward this improvement would have been extremely prejudicial, if not disastrous, to the true interests of the Company, in which the Commonwealth has the very large interest of 24,115 shares.

The undersigned have not thought, and do not now suppose, that the interest of the Railroad Company, of the City of Boston, or of the Commonwealth, would be promoted by the development and improvement of these flats far in advance and anticipation of any possible occasion for their use, but that all reasonable allowances would be made for the altered condition of things from that existing at the time of the execution of the contract. Although, if the purchase had not been made, it might be a question whether it would be a wise and judicious one to make at the present time, the Railroad Company do not ask to be relieved from their obligation to pay for said flats according to the true meaning and spirit of the contract; but, in view of all the circumstances, the undersigned, in behalf of said Railroad Company, propose to the Commissioners representing the Commonwealth as follows : —

The Boston and Albany Railroad Company shall pay to the Commonwealth on the first day of April next (which is assumed to be the time when the Commonwealth will have fully performed its work upon its area of flats adjoining and north-west of the flats of said Railroad Company), in cash, or in such other manner as shall be mutually agreed upon, the amount which shall be due to said Commonwealth for the flats to be conveyed to said Company, after making all due allowances and giving proper credits as hereinbefore stated.

That the Commnnwealth shall release said Railroad Company from all claim for interest on said purchase-money prior to said April 1, 1878.

That said Commonwealth shall give a deed of said flats, or other satisfactory acknowledgment of said payment.

That said Commonwealth shall not require said Railroad Company to go on with its work except in connection with improvements upon the flats of the Commonwealth lying east of those of said Railroad Company.

> C. W. CHAPIN.
> D. WALDO LINCOLN.
> IGNATIUS SARGENT.
> JOHN CUMMINGS.
> THOMAS TALBOT.

OFFICE OF THE LAND COMMISSIONERS,
STATE HOUSE, BOSTON, NOV. 30, 1877.

To Messrs. C. W. CHAPIN, D. WALDO LINCOLN, IGNATIUS SARGENT, JOHN CUMMINGS, and THOMAS TALBOT, *Committee of the Boston and Albany Railroad Company.*

The Board of Land Commissioners have the honor to acknowledge the receipt of your communication of the 1st inst., making propositions for the adjustment of the account between the Commonwealth and your Corporation arising from the purchase by your Company from the Commonwealth of a tract of land or flats, not less than fifty acres, in South Boston, in accordance with the agreement of December 8, 1869, as modified by the supplementary agreement of June 24, 1873.

And the Board notes, that if certain allowances, fully described in your communication, shall be assented to by the Commonwealth, your Company will be ready to pay to the Commonwealth, on the first day of April next, the sum of $330,476.

The Board has carefully examined the contracts of 1869 and 1873, and has given to your communication the fullest consideration, and now beg to submit to your Company its views of the stipulations of the said two agreements, and its reasons for the non-allowance of several items of account as claimed by your Company.

Under the agreement of December 8, 1868, your Company agreed to purchase of the Commonwealth fifty (50) acres of flats in South Boston, at the rate of twenty (20) cents per square foot. By the supplementary agreement of June 24, 1873, between the Commonwealth and your Company, your Company, in terms, surrendered to the Commonwealth all the flats purchased of the Commonwealth, and described in the agreement of December 8, 1869, lying south-west of the south-westerly line of Eastern Avenue, "except such portions of said flats as is to be conveyed to said Company, as hereinafter provided, for a road-bed for its tracks." It thus appears, that, in your surrender, you reserved an undefined area as a road-bed for tracks to be thereafter located.

By the same supplementary agreement, the Commonwealth agreed to convey to your Company, and your Company agreed to take, upon agreed terms, other lands "in place of and as an equivalent for such flats so surrendered;" and the parties mutually "agreed to define specifically, by metes and bounds, said strip, as soon as Eastern Avenue shall be located under said indenture of four parts." No such mutual defining by metes and bounds of the strip to be conveyed to your Company by the Commonwealth, as an equivalent for the area surrendered, has been had. An attempt to so define such area was initiated by the Harbor Commissioners, by an order as follows : —

"COMMONWEALTH OF MASSACHUSETTS.

"HARBOR COMMISSIONERS' OFFICE,
No. 8 PEMBERTON SQUARE, BOSTON, February 4, 1874.

" " At a meeting of the Board held this day, it was voted, that Mr. Whiting give the width of the strip of land along the southeast border of the Commonwealth's parcel of flats at the junction of Main and Fort Point Channels the Boston and Albany Railroad Company is to receive for the land surrendered by the Company south-west of the old location of Eastern Avenue.

. " A true copy.   Attest :

" (Signed) .   F. W. LINCOLN, *Chairman.*"

Under which order Mr. Whiting made a report, dated February 10, 1874, to the Board of Harbor Commissioners ; which report was never adopted by the Board, nor, so far as we are informed, accepted by your Company.

From an examination of said report of Mr. Whiting, submitted to the Board of Harbor Commissioners, it appears that it comprises two-fifths, not of the land, in fact, surrendered, but of your Company's original purchase lying south-westerly of Eastern Avenue. It appears, therefore, that your Company was not entitled to a strip of land ninety-six and a half feet wide, but only to a strip of such width as would be equal in area to two-fifths of the area surrendered by you.

How much your Company did not surrender can only be ascertained when the location of its road-bed forty feet wide is fixed. Then it will be possible to fix the width of the strip of land which shall be in area two-fifths of the area surrendered by your Company on June 24, 1873.

Although it is therefore still impossible to fix the boundaries of your territory on either side of Eastern Avenue, the amount of purchase-money remains the same as originally fixed in the contract of December 8, 1869, because the exchange of lands gives to your Company two-fifths as many feet at fifty cents per foot as the Commonwealth receives from your Company at twenty cents per foot. This amount was fixed at $438,600 in the agreement of December 8, 1869, and is the amount to be paid by your Company, less such reductions, if any, as it may be entitled to.

The agreement of 1869 contained certain stipulations as to payments and interest; but, as these were modified by the agreement of 1873, it is not necessary to refer to them now particularly.

On the 24th June, 1873, your Company entered into an agreement of four parts with the Commonwealth, the City of Boston, and the Boston Wharf Company, in which your Company agreed to fill and to enclose with a sea-wall upon the north-east side thereof, except the space required for docks, before the first day of October, 1876, the flats purchased by it of the Commonwealth; and on the same day your Company made a supplementary contract with the Commonwealth, wherein the Commonwealth agreed, in consideration of the stipulations entered into by your Company in the said agreement of four parts, to extend the time of payment of the $435,600, without interest, to October 1, 1876, and also agreed to deduct the cost of the heavy sea-wall to be built by your Company in front of the strip of land hereinbefore referred to, at the average cost per foot of the whole heavy sea-wall upon the north-east side of the territory purchased by it, and also to allow it to surrender any portion of its purchase which might remain south-west of the line of Eastern Avenue if finally located northerly of the line of location as described in the plan of 1869, and to reimburse it for one-half the cost paid by it for filling Eastern Avenue upon the south-west side of its purchase. In the contract of 1869, the Commonwealth reserved the right to locate Eastern Avenue and B Street extended, and in that event agreed to refund to your Company at the rate of twenty cents per foot for the land included within their locations.

Your Company has relinquished the piece of land lying south-westerly of the new location of Eastern Avenue, and is entitled to a credit therefor to the amount of $25,600. But the Land Commissioners fail to see that your Company *is now* entitled to any credit for the cost of the heavy sea-wall already built by your Company in front of the strip hereinbefore referred to, because your Company has not yet built the whole of the heavy sea-wall upon the north side of its purchase, and is therefore unable to fix the average cost per foot of the whole of said wall, and because, further, the length of the sea-wall for which your Company is to be so reimbursed is as yet undetermined.

The Land Commissioners also fail to see why your Company should now be allowed for the space to be included in Northern Avenue or B Street extended, because the Commonwealth has not yet and may never avail of its right to locate said avenue and street.

Nor do the Land Commissioners see the justice of now allowing to your Company one-half the estimated cost of filling Eastern Avenue, because your Company has not yet done the work, nor incurred "cost" for filling said avenue.

It is evident that the supplementary agreement of 1873 was drawn with the intention of providing that all work, both upon the twenty-five-acre piece belonging to the Commonwealth and upon the flats purchased by your Company, should be completed by the first day of October, 1876 ; that on that day the whole of the sea-wall upon your Company's exterior line should have been completed, and your Company's territory should have been all filled ; that Northern Avenue and the extension of B Street, if such avenue and street were decided upon, would have been located and laid out, and that Eastern Avenue upon the south-west boundary of your Company's land should have been filled by it ; that the location of its tracks south-west of Eastern Avenue would have been fixed, and that the width of the strip upon the northwest side of your Company's purchase would have been determined, so that a deed of the territory, described fully by metes and bounds, could have been given to your Company on that day by the Commonwealth, upon your Company's paying to the Commonwealth the sum of $435,600, less the following items ; viz., —

Cost of sea-wall in front of strip (exchanged) at average cost of your Company's whole wall   feet of land included in the location of Northern Avenue and B Street extended (if any) at 20c.   One-half the cost paid by your Company for filling Eastern Avenue, and square feet of land northerly of old line, and southerly of new line of Eastern Avenue (now fixed at 128,000 square feet), at 20c.

The amount of none of which, except the last, can now be ascertained.   And it was in pursuance of the interest of said agreement that a provision was made for the *deduction* from the sum agreed to be paid by your Company of the average cost in some cases, and the actual cost in others, and in others still a specific price per foot of land.

But it is evident, that, while the Commonwealth agreed to deduct for work when actually completed by your Company, it did not intend to deduct for estimated cost of work which your Company had agreed to do, but had not done ; and it agreed to deduct the average cost per foot of your Company's whole sea-wall for every foot built by it in front of the strip of land exchanged, but not the price paid by your Company for the wall built in front of said strip, unless your Company's whole wall was completed.

The object of the contract was to secure the filling of the territory purchased by your Company, the completion of the sea-wall, the filling of Eastern Avenue and B Street extended, and Northern Avenue, so that they could be used as an entrance upon, and an exit from, the twenty-five-acre piece of the Commonwealth by the first of October, 1876 ; and, as the inducements to the completion of your Company's work, it was agreed that its purchase-money should be without interest to October 1, 1876 ; and that, on that day, certain deductions for work already done by your Company should be made. And there was still another object which the Commonwealth had in securing the completion of your Company's work on that date, and for allowing so liberally in settlement of its account; and that was, the completion of Northern-Avenue Bridge by the City of Boston, which the city agreed to build in twelve months after the completion of the filling of your Company's, the Commonwealth's, and the Boston Wharf Company's territory. Until after your Company's flats are filled, the Commonwealth can have no direct avenue between its twenty-five-acre piece and the city proper, but will be obliged to reach it by the Eastern-Avenue bridge and A Street extended therefrom over the land of the Boston Wharf Company, which will add much to the distance, and, materially reduce the value of the Commonwealth's lands for docks and warehouses to be used in connection with the business of the city.

The account between the Commonwealth of Massachusetts and your Company stands as follows : —

THE BOSTON AND ALBANY RAILROAD COMPANY TO THE COMMONWEALTH OF MASSACHUSETTS, ... DR.

For 50 acres of land purchased in 1869 @ 20 cts. per sq. foot,	$435,600
Less 128,000 sq. feet south of the present location of Eastern Avenue, surrendered, @ 20 cts., ...	25,600
Due as cash October 1, 1876, as per agreement June 24, 1876, ...	$410,000
Interest on same from October 1, 1876, to . . .	–
	–

The amount due from your Company being thus found to be $410,000, with interest from October 1, 1876, the Commonwealth is asked to make no charge of interest from said last date to April 1, 1878, at which date you assume that the Commonwealth will have filled its territory lying north-west of your Company's purchase ; and your claim for the allowance rests entirely, so far as the Land Commissioners can see, upon the failure of the Commonwealth to complete its filling until the last-named date. In reply to the assumption that the filling of the Commonwealth's land north-west of your Company's purchase will not be completed before the first day of April, 1878, the Land Commissioners have the pleasure of announcing to you, that, so far as can now be ascertained, all the filling will be completed before the first day of January next; so that, if your proposition of allowance of interest and payment for your Company's purchase is to be fixed as due upon the filling of the Commonwealth's lands aforesaid, the allowance of interest should cease, and payment should be made on the first day of January next.

But the Land Commissioners fail to see any ground for your claim. The Commonwealth agreed to fill its above-described territory by the 1st of October, 1876, in the agreement of June 24, 1873, and, in anticipation of your Company's agreement to complete its filling at the same time, extended the time of the payment of its purchase-money without interest to the same date. The Commonwealth will have done all that it agreed to do within fifteen months of the date specified; while your Company, at the same date, will have done almost nothing towards completing the work which it agreed to finish on the 1st of October, 1876. To this proposition the Land Commissioners beg to say in reply, that they fail to find anywhere the power vested in them which permits them to make the allowance of interest which your Company desires. But, as soon as the items of the account between the Commonwealth and your Company are agreed upon, it will be the duty of the Board to notify the Governor and Council of your request; and that duty the Board will perform promptly.

In regard to the last proposition contained in your communication, the Land Commissioners have informed you verbally, and now beg to repeat, that as your agreement to complete its filling and walls is also included among the stipulations of the indenture of four parts, bearing date June 24, 1873, to which the Commonwealth was only one of the parties, it is out of their power, even if they so desired, to grant an extension of time for the completion of the work agreed to be done by your Company, or to still further agree that your Company need not go on with its filling, except as the Commonwealth shall hereafter fill to the south-east of your Company's purchase.

The Land Commissioners regret that they, with due regard to the rights and interest of the Commonwealth, have not been able to construe the contracts and agreements between your Company and the Commonwealth as you do, while they have desired to yield to your Company every thing to which it was fairly entitled. ·

The value of the property at South Boston can be best promoted by the harmonious action of all the parties interested ; and it will be the aim of the Land Commissioners, in their dealings with your Company, to aid, by every means in their power, the development of the whole property.

We are, gentlemen, yours respectfully,

> WILLARD P. PHILLIPS,
> EDWARD C. PURDY,
> HORACE C. BACON,
> *Land Commissioners.*

[Copy.]

OFFICE OF THE BOSTON AND ALBANY RAILROAD COMPANY, }
BOSTON, December 27, 1877. }

To HON. WILLARD P. PHILLIPS, EDWARD C. PURDY, HORACE C. BACON,
Land Commissioners.

The undersigned, a Committee of the Directors of the Boston and Albany Railroad Company, have the honor to acknowledge the receipt of your communication, dated November 30 last ; and, in reply thereto, respectfully submit for your consideration the grounds upon which they rest the claim of the Company for the allowances which they asked for.

The Committee notice what the Commissioners have said in relation to the undefined area which is to be conveyed to the Railroad Company for a road-bed across the strip of flats of the Commonwealth lying south-west of Eastern Avenue.

This strip of flats is about 720 feet in length, 150 feet wide at its widest, and 70 feet wide at its narrowest end. If it should be crossed midway by the proposed railroad, the road-bed would occupy an area 110 feet by 40 feet, or 4,400 square feet, which, at 20 cents a foot, would cost $880. If this area should be exchanged for other land of the Commonwealth, as proposed, in the proportion of five feet for two, the area to be received from the Commonwealth, bounded south-easterly by the flats sold to the Railroad Company under the agreement of December 8, 1869, will be reduced 1,760 feet. As the strip of land received from the Commonwealth in said exchange is about 1,300 feet in length, the deduction of 1,760 feet will lessen its width $1\frac{354}{1000}$ feet only, reducing it from $96\frac{1}{2}$ feet to about $95\frac{1}{6}$ feet.

Inasmuch as the Railroad Company have not secured a right of
way over any portion of the route between their railroad and the
South Boston Flats, and as it is entirely undetermined in what
manner these flats can be reached, if at all, by rail, the right to
this undefined area for a road-bed can be released by the Railroad
Company to the Commonwealth, without prejudice to the interests
of either party. Such a release will be given if it is desired by
the Commissioners.

The agreement by which the parties mutually engaged to define
by metes and bounds the strip of flats to be taken from the Commonwealth, as an equivalent for the flats surrendered by the Railroad Company, is not understood by the Committee to bind the
Railroad Company to join or aid in the surveys or measurements
of said area. The Commonwealth has a special Board of Commissioners, who are thoroughly acquainted with all the property,
and charged with its care and management. They have skilful
engineers in their service, and all the plans relating to the property
in their custody. The Railroad's officials have no such means and
facilities for acting in the premises. The Company interpreted
this clause in the contract to mean, that, after this area had been
surveyed and determined by the engineers of the Harbor Commissioners, the parties should mutually join in "defining the metes
and bounds" by the establishment of permanent monuments to
mark the boundaries. The Commissioners will please notice that
the vote of the Harbor Commissioners, referred to in their communication directing their engineer, Mr. Whiting, to "give the
width of the strip," did not direct him to ask the co-operation of
the engineer of the Railroad Company. The Committee are also
informed that said vote was never communicated to the officers of
the Railroad Company, — a fact of which they do not complain, as
they see no reason why it should have been communicated to them.
The Railroad Company will now instruct their engineers to join in
making said surveys, if it is desired by the Commissioners.

The Committee have reason to believe that the allowance for
the cost of the heavy sea-wall, for which they now make claim,
was provided for in the supplementary contract of June 24, 1873,
because, in the exchange of flats, the Railroad Company surrendered an area south-west of Eastern Avenue, which did not require
a sea-wall, in exchange for a smaller area, at a much higher price,
which did require it, thus relieving the Commonwealth from the
burden of building and maintaining a portion of the heavy sea-
wall, which it must otherwise have built. This wall has now been
entirely constructed and paid for by the Railroad Company, and, as

the Committee understand, for the whole 96½ feet, or by the construction of the dock and light wall as a substitute for a portion of it; and the Commonwealth has been enabled thereby to fill its entire area of twenty-five acres, which it could not otherwise have done: but it so happens, that it cannot now be determined, in the particular manner in which it was provided in the contract, what the exact allowance for the sea-wall shall be. For the purpose of the present settlement, the Committee have charged the price actually paid by the Commonwealth for its wall of the same dimensions and description, under contracts awarded, after competition, to the lowest bidder, at a period of unexampled depression in the price of labor and materials. The contracts made by the Railroad Company were with the same parties who contracted with the Commonwealth, and for the same price. The cost of the wall yet to be built, it is quite probable, will be greater, rather than less, than the price already paid.

The Committee understand the Commissioners to admit the claim of the Railroad Company to an allowance for the area included within the limits of Northern Avenue, when it shall have been located, but suggest that the Commonwealth may never locate said avenue. In another part of their communication, the Commissioners have spoken of the importance of this avenue to the development of the property of the Commonwealth, to which the Committee respectfully call their attention.

They also respectfully refer the Commissioners to the clause in the Indenture of four parts, dated June 24, 1873, wherein the Commonwealth agreed with the City of Boston to fill a certain portion of its flats within the limits of Northern Avenue, and also agreed that the city may lay out said avenue without incurring liability for land damages.

The obligation of the Commonwealth and of the Railroad in relation to the filling of Eastern Avenue are substantially the same. A communication has been addressed to the Land Commissioners and to the Railroad Company by the Board of Aldermen of the City of Boston, dated November 5 last, in which both parties are requested to fulfil their agreements concerning Eastern Avenue. Their obligations to the city under the Indenture of June, 1873, will probably require them to fill a portion of that avenue during the next year.

The Committee respectfully ask the Commissioners to accept the obligation of the Railroad Company, with security, if desired, to fill said avenue *pari passu*, or in co-operation with the Commonwealth, each doing its portion of the work, instead of requiring the payment of a considerable sum of money by the Railroad Company, to be afterwards refunded by the Commonwealth with interest.

The Committee note, that the Commissioners in their communication assume that the Railroad Company, by the Indenture of December 8, 1869, agreed to purchase and pay for fifty acres of flats at the rate of twenty cents per square foot, and now owe for the entire fifty acres.

By that contract, the Commonwealth agreed to convey to the Railroad Company, not fifty acres, but a certain area of flats specifically defined by metes and bounds. Included within that area, and mäking part of it, were portions of Northern and Eastern Avenues and B Street, which were to be conveyed to the Company, but without compensation. By the allowances for the areas included within these avenues and streets, by the exchanges which have been made, and by the abandonment of 128,000 feet lying south-west of Eastern Avenue, the area to be paid for has been reduced, according to the statement of the engineer of the Harbor Commissioners, to about 1,653,524 feet, or $37\frac{959}{1000}$ acres, of whioh 126,984 feet are to be paid for at 50 cents a foot, and the remainder at 20 cents.

The agreement of the Railroad Company to pay the sum of $435,600 is qualified by the condition, that the territory shall be surveyed by the engineers of the Board of Harbor Commissioners, and said sum shall be increased or diminished, according as said area, exclusive of that portion of it which is within the limits of Northern and Eastern Avenues and B Street, shall be found to be more or less than fifty acres. The contract provides that said territory shall be surveyed when it shall have been filled; but there is nothing to prohibit or prevent the survey from being made before the completion of the filling, if the interests of the parties, for the purpose of effecting a settlement and securing the payment of the purchase-money, require it to be done.

The Committee respectfully ask the Commissioners to consider if the survey contemplated in the contract cannot.be made at the present time, in order to determine the quantity of flats to be conveyed to and paid for by the Railroad Company.

If this survey can be now made, the Committee trust that a satisfactory arrangement can be made with the Commissioners, by which the Commonwealth can be secured against any possible contingency of loss on account of the allowances for the road-bed across the area south-west of Eastern Avenue, for the price of the heavy sea-wall, and for the filling of Eastern Avenue.

The Committee acquiesce in the decision of the Commissioners to refer the matter of the allowance of interest to the Governor and Council. They also concede the point made by the Commissioners, that it is not in their power to change the terms of the supplementary contract of June 24, 1873, in which other parties are interested.

We are, gentlemen, yours very respectfully,

C. W. CHAPIN,
D. WILDO LINCOLN,
JOHN CUMMINGS,
IGNATIUS SARGENT,
THOMAS TALBOT,
FRANCIS B. HAYES,
Committee.

MEMORANDA OF POINTS AT ISSUE BETWEEN THE LAND COMMISSIONERS AND THE BOSTON AND ALBANY RAILROAD.

1. Settlement in regard to the forty feet for road-bed for tracks south of Eastern Avenue not surrendered by Boston and Albany Railroad in 1873. Commonwealth proposes to accept said surrender upon condition of surrender of contract rights to lay tracks on Commonwealth's land, and across Eastern Avenue, at grade; and Commonwealth will allow two-fifths of the area of forty feet in width in exchange, as by indenture of 1873.

2. Question of access to, and egress from, twenty-five-acre lot, of which Commonwealth is deprived through delay of Boston and Albany Railroad in filling their land. How can State secure exit as valuable? and how can State be compensated for loss of use of Northern-Avenue Bridge, and the extension of A Street?

3. If allowance for areas of Northern Avenue and B Street extended shall be allowed, then, for present adjustment, Northern Avenue to be settled as seventy-five feet wide, and B Street extended as fifty feet wide, subject to extra allowance to Boston and Albany Railroad, if City of Boston lays out said street and avenue at a greater width, as provided in contract of 1873.

4. Eastern Avenue to be filled, as it is required to be, under agreement of four parts: Commonwealth to pay its half as work progresses if appropriation can be secured in time; if not, as soon as the same can secured; contract for said filling to be assented to and approved by said Land Commissioners.

5. Commonwealth to pay Boston and Albany Railroad at the rate paid them in the contract for constructing sea-wall in front of strips exchanged; Commonwealth waiving the right to compel the construction of the whole sea-wall before settlement, but not waiving any right to compel its construction as provided in the contract of 1869, as modified by contract of 1873.

[COPY.]

[CITY SEAL.]   EXECUTIVE DEPARTMENT, CITY HALL, }
Mayor's Office.   BOSTON, Nov. 23, 1877.   }

To the Land Commissioners of the Commonwealth : —

GENTLEMEN, — Your early attention is respectfully directed to the order of the City Council passed November 8, 1877, a duly attested copy of which is enclosed.

Very respectfully
Your obedient servant,

FREDERICK O. PRINCE, *Mayor.*

[COPY.]

CITY OF BOSTON, IN BOARD OF ALDERMEN, }
            November 5, 1877.   }

Ordered, That the Board of Land Commissioners, acting for the Commonwealth of Massachusetts, be requested to commence forthwith the building of B Street or C Street, from First Street to Eastern Avenue, and to complete the same as soon as practicable, in accordance with an indenture between the Commonwealth of Massachusetts, the Boston and Albany Railroad, the Boston Wharf Company, and the City of Boston, dated June 24, 1873 ; and also that the said Commissioners, in case they should elect to build C Street instead of B Street, be requested to build that portion of Eastern Avenue lying between the easterly line of flats belonging to the Boston and Albany Railroad Company and the easterly line of said C Street, in accordance with said indenture ; and that the Boston and Albany Railroad Company be requested to fill to grade sixteen feet above mean low water that portion of Eastern Avenue that is embraced within the limits of the flats purchased by said Company of the said Commonwealth of Massachusetts, also in accordance with said indenture.

Passed, sent down for concurrence, November 8. Came up concurred.

Approved by the Mayor November 12, 1877.

A true copy.

Attest: S. F. McCLEARY, *City Clerk.*

8